55 FACES
Global Edition

The Aspire Series

Copyright © Michelle Gardiner 2023

First published in Australia in 2023
by KMD Books
Waikiki, WA 6169

All rights reserved. No part of this book may be used or reproduced by any means, graphic, electronic, or mechanical, including photocopying, recording, taping or by any information storage retrieval system without the written permission of the copyright owner except in the case of brief quotations embodied in critical articles and reviews.

Because of the dynamic nature of the Internet, any web addresses or links contained in this book may have changed since publication and may no longer be vaild. The views expressed in this work are solely those of the author and do not necessarily reflect the views of the publisher and the publisher hereby disclaims any responsibility for them.

 A catalogue record for this work is available from the National Library of Australia

National Library of Australia Catalogue-in-Publication data:

55 Faces: Global Edition/Michelle Gardiner

ISBN: 978-0-6456765-9-4 (Paperback)

'It takes a while to develop a voice. But once you have it, you damn sure better use it on stuff that matters.' – Oprah Winfrey

With my deepest gratitude:

To my current mentor, Suzana Mihajlovic of *Your 2 Minds,* for your endless support, encouragement and divine intervention, and my previous mentor, Susan Santoro, who helped to fertilise what has become *The Aspire Series*.

To every woman presented in this book, thank you eternally for sharing your heart, words, energy and lives with me. It is my dream that this book can create a little more space for you to live your own dreams more fully.

Finally, women do best in the world when supported by men and the masculine. For this, I wish to acknowledge and thank the following men for their support of me through this project: Tarek Kholoussy of Nomads Giving Back for opening doorways that welcomed several women into this project, George Bossous Junior for his dear friendship and my father, Robert Gardiner, for holding his own despite his daughter's harebrained ideas.

To those who inspire me and feed my spirit 'from up above':

My maternal grandmother, Margaret Andrews, who taught me to love fully, wholeheartedly and tirelessly.

My dear friend, Tina Vercillo, I know you would have been the first woman to be in this book and my number-one supporter throughout this project.

Contents

Foreword 1
Prelude 9
Women's letter 15
   Melanie Ryan 21
   Agnes Appiah Apawu 27
   Sarah Rapp 33
   Nettie Floyd 39
   Rachel De Summa 45
   Stephanie Hoo 51
   Suzana Mihajlovic 57
   Isotta Rossoni 63
   Toni Lontis 69
   Catherine Shovlin 75

Kim Bleeze 81
Maria Boulatsakos 87
Marcelle Rouchon 93
Cate Dubois 99
Rina Mittiga 105
Laura Coburn 111
Asia Raine 117
Jenny Chiu 123
Bianca Caruana 129
Anne Carr 135
Stephanie Siefkas 141
Kylie Butler 147
Penelope Joy 153
Mandy Terbrueggen 159
Julie Scollary 165
Camille R Francis 171
Ambra Cristaldi 177
Komal Kaur 183
Erin Cotter-Smith 189
Nadia Pace 195
Trudy Morter 201
Michelle Poole 207
Mary Deng-Crisp 213
Bianca Raby 219
Kylie L Clarke 225
Tania Russell 231

Yasmine Walker 237
Penelope Prana 243
Laura Morrice 249
Gaelyn Miriam Larrick 255
Sharon Chemello 261
Charlott Kisvarda 267
Erin Pintar 273
Jinju Dasalla 279
Vicki Lark 285
Viviana Premazzi 291
Christina Fletcher 297
Mea Allman 303
Karli Bree 309
Megan Rose 315
Michelle Berger 321
Nathalie Banaszak 327
Lisa Cybaniak Gustafsson 333
Gail Carmody 339
Jasmine Gatt 345
Epilogue 351

Foreword

by Francesca Fondse
From: South Africa

Today, I own my knowledge as a person of substance. A woman.

Dear sisters and fellow souls,

A lot of ponderance preceded my reach to you, in your totality, as I am expressing me to you, and turn to my being-ness in this world, but to paint a written picture to you, that you will surely bathe my lament in the hues of your own understanding. That is reach. That is how this is supposed to be. Today, I am speaking to sisters, women who have defined their journeys and humans who hold space for the next generations to come. I can only express as me, and thus, as a woman who lived and in that living encountered the worst of man, in subtle, communal and personal ways, my wish would be for men to read these revelations, as it would take all of us to negate and conform the challenges which face the human condition and transform to the humane reality.

My story started more than half a century ago, on a farm in Africa … It would become the story of a little girl with white hair who would sing opera to nature and run along dusty farm roads. A girl who had very little knowledge of self in their rather large family, and direct contact with her mother only came because of a fatal disease. Yet, their conversations during this painful time as death winged closer would shape her life choices in so many ways. Our mother passed away soon after. I was twelve years old. Her death left me neglected, as the age gap between siblings was widened by her passing, and my older siblings were centred in their own mourning.

Strangers became guidance, which was not available in our family. The lady at the pharmacy consoled me when I encountered the onset of 'womanhood'. Truly, I did not 'fit' since birth, and my 'weirdness' was a source of challenge within family and societal context. My spirit questioned the consequentiality of our daily actions, our humanity and our purpose, which in turn conflicted with ideologies, both political and religious. I have loved. Deeply. And I know the malady of loss. And abandonment. I have experienced the depths and torments of betrayal, in love and from family … Those who are supposed to be our shelter.

It was my choices, my focus and my deep knowledge that strengthened my convictions. And became the armour that would shield my mind and my soul from the onslaughts which were apparent. The body, however, suffered at times. But it also experienced the blessings of love and womanhood. The joys of harbouring a growing child in the womb and the pains of labour.

The ebbs and flow of my life saw me revolt against inhumanity, delve into the vast cosmos of mysticism, and finally, challenged by a divorce which was as destructive as the plagues of Egypt. But one suffices, and you get up and get through the day. And you keep on getting up and refocus yourself until getting up is rising! And then you start making the impossible possible. You get to truly inhabit your body, and you get to love your seen and invisible scars, as they comprise all of you.

Throughout the centuries, women were called upon to be strong, to be unseen architects of society, to be mothers, objects of infatuation, to be portrayed as whores when it suited the narrative, the damsels in distress, to highlight the strength of a 'saviour' in a man etc. Men and women were raised in expectations which did not correlate to sacred scriptures or reality. Should we investigate all the related ideologies pertaining to the origins of man, it reveals to me that women are strength itself, whilst traditionally, a man was seen to be her protector. Yet, to my understanding, a marriage, in whichever form it may take, has always been assigned to partnership. We need to get back to a value system of balance.

Today, I own my knowledge as a person of substance. A woman. After facing political violence and many forms of relational violence, within my family, relationships and marriage, it has become clear that humanity is at the precipice of redefining these conditions, and that we can aspire to the love portrayed in fairytales, but there is a vast need to raise our children with the understanding that after the choice, arise sequential daily choices, which all bear consequences! That it is only through dedication and commitment that there is in fact a happy ending possible. Through common sense, communication and heart-centred collaboration, we can have happy relationships, we can raise consequentialist thinkers and we can steer humanity towards peaceful and even delightful shared lives. But it takes consideration and willingness to change. It takes vision.

The women whose stories are featured in this book all have lived. Some, better than others. But ultimately, all lives offer the opportunity to gaze within, to assess and to gather information which could be helpful to your own journey. We may all learn from one another. Lessons all speak to humanity, personal relations and ultimately human dignity and freedom! Truly, when we look at global, national and interpersonal conflicts, they all speak to those. Dignity, relations and freedom of expression, or freedom of being who we are! Add a touch of commitment and love, and we may endure challenges and find joy in doing so. I know the challenges of losing a home, of not knowing how to provide for the next meal and afford nappies. The flowers upon my life were soaked in many tears but strengthened through perseverance.

It is my sincere wish that all women will find their voice, their dignity of self-expression, of choice. To be educated to make choices, to be informed and to feel empowered. To be informed of the consequentiality of life and our expressions. To feel valued for our contribution, to live free of insinuation and oppression and to thrive. May your minds and your hearts smile simultaneously many times within your lives!

The little barefoot girl grew up, faced her share of demons, and finally, though a bit battle-worn, finally found her 'SELF'. And I can assess my impact on the political landscape of my country, the empowerment of women and gender awareness and my gifts. Amongst these will be my books, but my crowning joy are my children. I raised consequential persons, and I am certain they will continue the same. However, self-acceptance comes from self-awareness which is followed by self-forgiveness. We must unload the burdens of past mistakes when we were ill-equipped to deal with our journeys. And we must forgive those who came before us, our ancestors, our teachers, our fathers especially, and understand that we are the ones who unlock the bondage of societal and generational ignorance.

Yes, many journeys are entwined with themes of global violence, wars and tribal or ethnic conflicts, might deal with domestic violence, childhood traumas, spiritual awakening, moving from desperation to entrepreneurship, willing and unprepared roles of leadership, significant life changes, whether economical, medical, psychological challenges or whichever way induced. We need to start taking steps, no matter how small, towards health, mental wellbeing and finding our voice. Stumble if you must, but start!

One can recover from physical, emotional, sexual, psychological and economic abuse. Through finding help, through collaboration and mutual understanding, we may heal. It is essential to understand that we all harbour traumas which scream for healing and plead for recovery. May this work be an inspiration to change, to expression and to new choices.

We need to detangle the complexities of human behaviour, through honesty. We can undo the structural, ideological and institutionalised violent complexities within societal constructs towards gender roles. We can stop economic exploitation, patriarchal violence and judicial victimisation. We – general society – are responsible for the normalisation of behaviours that hurt us, through our attitudes and conscription. We must investigate the discourses of our morality, redefine our expectations and determine new values. We are responsible for enduring the social, actual and mental poverty, which leads to discord. We need to engage our traditions, our environment and our customs and purge those of practices that are harmful to the wellbeing of future generations. WE need to be the change we wish to see!

Women should engage their sisterhood. We should support each other. Champion our joint goodness and vision of an educated, peaceful humanity. We are the birthers of all. Our success or failure ultimately starts with us. May the stars shine ever brighter for you, and may your feet find favour upon your journey … Should tears fall upon your cheeks, may flowers grow and bloom upon your life. May our dreams align, your heart find its fire and the future unfold with splendour, because we are.

With love and light,
Francesca Fondse

Woman, mother, mystic, author, professional, business entrepreneur, Impact Project specialist and UNGC member.

Founder of Women Integral Impact Network (WIIN) and co-founder International Community for Domestic Peace (ICFDP).

Member of global empowerment organisations, wellness empowerment institutions and research structures.

National champion for women, Department of Justice and Constitutional Development, South Africa.

Prelude

by Michelle Gardiner

37 | From: Melbourne, Australia | Lives: Bali, Indonesia

You see the dichotomy of space between each woman as mother, daughter, sister, healer, leader, feeler, activist and creator. In this tender space, when we draw on our lived wisdom, and come together, we open a potent alchemy for change. In this space, we see every woman ultimately as both a leader and healer, holding the seeds to help us all.

Hello, wonderful human!

I would firstly like to share my deepest gratitude to you for picking up this copy of *55 FACES*. I will do my best to articulate in words what this means to me and the many women whose words are presented here.

Around a year ago, I asked for a miracle. I threw my hands up in the air, decided to let go and with little else ado, I asked for guidance. It was a very brave moment that was the beginning of big creativity. *55 FACES* was one of these, initially presented as a simple social media piece, it has expanded into two books, each highlighting over fifty-five women and the social impact arm of *The Aspire Series*. As a social worker, coach, narrative therapist and yoga teacher who has spent over sixteen years exploring, supporting and enabling others to rewrite their stories and to share these to facilitate broader impact and change, *55 FACES* has been a natural slip into expanded leadership that I have absolutely adored.

With a focus on both global and local change and impact, *55 FACES* offers its women the opportunity to contribute to both. Change is most effective when viewed through the lens of how micro communities interrelate with the macro and vice versa. We can see many similarities and themes when we look inward to our own stories and identities, as when we look at the broader picture of the societies that we create and exist within.

There are 115 women involved in the 2022 editions of *55 FACES*, with the global edition highlighting the stories, experiences and perspectives of women from more than ten countries, and the Bali/Indonesia version highlighting women mostly from

Bali but also several other areas of Indonesia. There is power in numbers and in standing together, sharing our words, wisdom and truth that offers us the chance to be powerful on our own and even stronger when brought together.

55 FACES brings power, beauty, grace, humility and honesty to the forefront while offering the women involved the opportunity to really question and define who they are, how they want to be seen, what they desire for the broader collective, what they want to create for themselves and how they wish to lead change. The process of compiling their pieces holds a story within itself of how each woman has overcome, shifted and grappled with herself and her circumstances to ensure that not only does every word shared count in its entirety, but that she is also proud to put her name and face to them.

In recognition of the lands that we pay our ancestry to and those that we step foot on, these too form a part of *55 FACES,* as recognition of their vital part of who we become in this world, as much as the broad diversity of ages, cultural heritage and social demographics found here.

I am often told that the women highlighted through *55 FACES* are strong. Each is an everyday woman who is prepared to ask the simple yet big and deep questions that draw our true richness to the surface for the world to see. We are impacted by the way that we reflect on each woman in a way that we, too, are changed.

It is my wish that within *55 FACES* you will see the dichotomy of space between each woman as mother, daughter, sister, healer, leader, feeler, expander, activist and creator. In this tender space, when we draw on our lived wisdom and come together, we open a potent alchemy for change. In this space, we see every woman ultimately as both a leader and healer, holding the seeds to help us all. *55 FACES* allows each woman to experience this within herself, and for the world to highlight her in this way. And so, *55 FACES* becomes both an activator and amplifier of what was already there to begin with.

It is my intention that *55 FACES* is a conversation starter where we can navigate the 'in-between space' of you and me a little more fluidly, generously and graciously. We know that this is a pivotal and transformative time, and it is essential that women are at the forefront of this, pursuing a kinder, gentler way of leading, existing, raising and expanding, using the best of our intuitive, loving and healing essence to carry the world forward.

These three simple questions have so much to say about the foundation of how we came to be in this moment and the experiences that have qualified our ideas and opinions of the world, as much as they are a statement for the world we are now contributing to.

And what is the story that I next want written for women?

It is the one of possibility, opportunity and support, where every single woman can access these spaces knowing her deservingness in them and her differences only ever enhance her capacity to contribute to the women beside her. It is the one where we honour intuition as strongly as any other form of decision-making and know, without a doubt, that we are safe to trust this, and ourselves, in following our true north. It is the one where true empowerment is in bringing all genders closer together, one day forgetting that there was ever any weakness that took centre stage from who we truly are.

It is the one where our truth lies in opening ourselves up to more deeply understand both the beautiful and crunchy parts of who and how we are, knowing there is forever a way through that will strengthen the humanity inside us all. It is the one of home, where these human vessels belong to us and are both our safe place and greatest birthers of joy, presence and love. It is the one where we truly understand that our defining parts are the exact medicinal concoction of a better world.

Imagine if these were the stories we heard from birth and imagine the world we would live in. Imagine what would become possible and what would co-create.

And what do I next want to write for myself?

I am already deep in the rewriting of my new story, and I express so much gratitude to be here. It is this, and it is this in amplified form. My interpretation of my own story and my gifts and skills when harnessed have meant that I serve best when drawing the light and wisdom out in others. My desire is to cultivate magic from this place and to assist women on their own journey in using the best of their own wisdom to create change in their communities. I want this globally for women in positions of high influence, as much as I want it for women in local communities who may not otherwise have this chance.

Personally, I deeply desire my own close-knit family unit, who are colourful, diverse and unique, bonded by blood or through the way our eyes see the world. There is no difference in these forms of human connection and love. We come together and our deep bonds co-create a quality, beautiful, nurturing and loving home. I live in a local community where I contribute the best of myself, feel deeply connected and that the best of myself is cherished, as I, too, cherish those who share this geographical plot of land and the gifts it affords.

Lastly, I anticipate a life of expanded movement, learning, love and the cultivation of something far greater than where we have all come from. Something that is innate and yet which we each remind one another to return to, over and over again.

It is my greatest dream that you thoroughly enjoy both the richness and diversity of these books and each woman here, taking onboard the threads of courage, wisdom, strength, love and generosity of spirit that you are presented with.

Love, magic and best wishes,
Michelle Gardiner
Founder, director and creator
The Aspire Series
55 FACES

Women's letter

Empowerment is knowing that each person in the world matters. There is so much going on that we can think 'does it even matter what I do?' This is beyond empowerment, it's a deeper understanding that our individual selves do make an impact. Every drop in the ocean is a part of the greater whole.

Beautiful reader,

We are delighted to present this book where we share with you stories and reflections of who we are in the world and what we wish for ourselves, other women and those who identify as women.

We represent wisdom from ten countries, numerous home nationalities and heritages and are aged between twenty-four and seventy-four years with varying lifestyles. Some of us are digital nomads bouncing across the world, some of us are humanitarians leading social enterprises, coaches, healers, artists, mothers, conversation and space holders and those strongly connected to spirit. Our common thread is that we are all women who see a better world and have a strong desire and passion to lead the way forward. We have lived a lot, we are smart, brave, huge hearted and determined.

Some of us are well-versed in sharing ourselves with the world, others have overcome huge limiting beliefs to reach this point. This has spurred us into action! We have released and transcended stories that once were our truth and defined the stories to carry us forward. Through amplifying our self-view and our capacity to rewrite stories, we provide support to others.

Through sharing our stories, we hope to empower our readers. We know what it is to overcome, as much as we know what it is to celebrate our own and others' glory. We care about community, and we know that women coming together, lifting one another up and collaborating can instigate positive change.

We believe in the power of a story and that sharing stories can influence change. It is through seeing yourself in me, that you, too, will evolve. Just as much as I will evolve through seeing myself in you. You will find hints and clues scattered through our stories that help pave the way forward, individually and collectively.

It is our intention that you will feel connected to our honesty, love, hope, inspiration, joy, wholeness, a sense of synergy, possibility, curiosity, synchronicity, magic, unity, empowerment, resonance and the capacity to create change as you see the world through our eyes for a moment. As we remember that as women, we not only create life, but we also ignite our power when brought together. We offer you the opportunity to see the world through new eyes and a broader perspective, feeling the vibration of truth that you, too, are here to live on purpose.

The messages that we carry and wish for you to take away are:

As women, we mother, and we also make a difference.

We are here in diversity and unity. We are all here together as much as we are offering our unique selves to the world.

Our voices create change.

We are a web of support for one another.

Here is a connection to the divine feminine.

We can overcome, we can heal … and we can tell our stories.

Ultimately, we are not defined by our history.

We all come from different walks of life and different lands, but at the core of this we are all connected and share the same essence.

The creation of this book created powerful connections between the authors. The process triggered unanticipated personal growth and empowerment. Some words from contributors include:

'If only my brother could see this. The more that we tell our stories, the more that we can create the space for men to do the same. We want to be of benefit and an inspiration to men as much as other women.'

'Empowerment is knowing that each person in the world matters. There is so much going on that we can think, *Does it even matter what I do?* This is beyond empowerment; it's a deeper understanding that our individual selves do make an impact. Every drop in the ocean is a part of the greater whole.'

'We all have stories of trauma and pain, but they do not define us. The ways that we choose to grow through our journey and make a positive impact in the way we help others is what matters.'

'There is vulnerability in telling the parts of our story. I feel "normal" for sharing and being able to say, "I've been through that too and it's okay to talk about it. I'm going to walk with you."'

'This is a web of womanhood where our resonance means that we can find ourselves in one another.'

We use our history to create our next HERstory.

As a result of this project, we would like to see people reach out, make connections and understand that we are better together. Through educating and informing, we hope to ignite a spark for new ways of being, creating possibilities, new conversations and the acceptance of both self, our lives, experiences and our spaces of connection and difference. This is a space where shame, fear and playing small is healed as we embrace stepping into the unknown, becoming inspired to embark on far broader dreams. *55 FACES* has further fed us in our work in how we assist others in also harnessing their power and together creating better for humanity.

It has been a blessing to support our Balinese and Indonesian friends and sisters to also share their stories, wisdom and culture through *55 FACES*. In the rawness of both our beauty and pain, we now have the potential to improve our reality.

Like a women's circle evolved, permission and space has been created that isn't so often found in the world. As our witnesses, we hope that you, too, have the pleasure of feeling connected to us, our lives, our essence and sense of oneness. And that you also feel moved to create change in ways that hold the deepest meaning for you.

Yours in love,
On behalf of the Global 55

Melanie Ryan

51 | From: Melbourne, Australia | Lives: Melbourne, Australia

Choose love over fear.

Creating a new earth occurs in every moment we provide a boy with an opportunity to articulate their emotions rather than shutting them down, as much as it is in creating reverence for women, and balance for us all.

This is who I am in the world …

I'm Mel, Melanie, Milly or Melza. Although these names have been given to me by the people I love, there is waaayyy more to ME. I feel like saying I'm not from Melbourne, I'm from the universe. So passionately connected to humans, being divided by country feels unnatural.

It nourishes me to serve and contribute as a mum, grandmother, friend, sister, lover and colleague. Aristotle said that, 'There is no modern sense of self, rather a soul that perceives, thinks and nourishes.' We are nourished through our thoughts, our sense of self and perceptions which are coloured by our life experiences and the roles we play.

Life is what happens to us, and we face our identity along the way, and when rocked or shaken, the universe says, 'You are not this or that thing, humble back, sweetheart.' There are significant moments that tap us on the shoulder in a huge way, demand we pay attention and when we take our hats off, we soften and open to the beauty awaiting us.

I see myself as fifteen years old, as a brand-new mum and as coming into the crone archetype holding wisdom of the generations, and still, I am the interpretation of how others show up when I show up lovingly.

The third of four kids born while my dad was in Vietnam serving in the Navy, I never felt heard or seen, and as long as I was shiny and sweet, I was loved (hold up,

I was always loved) and accepted … If any negative feelings came up, they were shut down. Brushing it under the carpet and never speaking was the birthing of my very skilled people pleaser. She travelled with me through school and every relationship. I lovingly broke free at forty-two years of age.

I met my husband – my soulmate – when I was eleven years old, and we started dating when we were fifteen. I first became a mother at twenty-two years old, and the second time at twenty-eight. I truly believed that I was a woman raising strong women, until my husband's suicide eleven years ago. My twelve-year-old had a doting relationship with her dad, and my older daughter, six weeks away from turning eighteen, was ready to join the Navy, buy her first car and join her dad for her first beer. Three very different perspectives of loss.

We experienced fear and trauma following my husband's death, and I held my older daughter's anger with a desire to save her from it. When I instead began showing up lovingly for her, she softened and could feel her emotions rather than projecting them. Oprah Winfrey and Bruce Perry's *What Happened to You?* taught me about trauma wisdom, and I now apply this in my work in mental health. I now appreciate the unforeseen gift my husband imparted upon me: self-determination. While unchosen, it strengthened my resolve to live authentically.

My sense of self has since changed enormously. I can say, 'Wowwww! Look at me now!' as I witness how my experiences have nourished me, increased my self-esteem and my capacity to love, give and serve.

This is the next story I want written for women ...

I want women to know who they are from a place of deep love, experiencing a 'welcome home to self', celebrating the wisdom of the generations without taking on the trauma and wounds. I want women to be able to get on a train without thinking, *If I sit there, am I safe?* I want women to know how to ask for their needs to be met.

I want every woman to experience laughter, joy and deep heart connections with all humans, not just other women. I want this for mothers, daughters, teenagers and little girls. I want this for women who don't want to be mothers, women who are unable to be mothers and for women who want six kids.

I want women to look after their health because it feels good, not because they feel like they HAVE to look good. I want women to rediscover their sexuality. I want women to hold their space in a room full of men without being afraid.

I want to connect with the older women of our generation, the crones who are postmenopause. I want women to fully appreciate that we fucking create life and deserve reverence!

This is the next story I am writing for myself ...

My story returns to connection, knowing that together we are more through our capacity to link arms across the planet, from the newest born baby girl to the oldest woman on the planet, we can drive braver conversations. I say this not from excluding men, but from honouring our differences and being able to invite them in.

The next part of my story, while the 'doing' aspect has not yet revealed itself, will be about how I open my heart further and have it seen. I've explored studying psychology or speaking on worldwide stages, and although I could enjoy these things immensely, women's circles, grassroots work, rattling the cages, breaking the boundaries in clinical settings and seeing the human inside, speak to my heart.

I love epic conversations with my daughters that break generational blocks. My own mother would put on a fake smile, refusing to speak about what is uncomfortable. I will not let my daughters drive their futures from these wounds, waiting until they are forty to figure it out. Watching my daughter leave an abusive relationship, I saw the bravery this took as she found her place in this world and grew new feathers in her wings.

Transforming generations to create a new earth matters to me. It's happening when my eight-year-old grandson reaches out to me after being bullied at school, together we sit on the floor with his head on my lap and he tells me his fears. It's when he gets upset over putting his pyjamas on and I intercept his mother – my daughter – before she reacts so that we can ask him why he is upset and he tells us that he feels humiliated that he is the only person who has to put pyjamas on while everyone else is dressed.

Creating a new earth occurs in every moment we provide a boy with an opportunity to articulate their emotions rather than shutting down, as much as it is in creating reverence for women and balance for us all.

Agnes Appiah Apawu

38 | From: Ghana | Lives: Gatineau, QC, Canada

I am a thriving survivor, a warrior, a child of Twereduap n Nyame (the God I can lean on) with a spirit that cannot be tamed.

This is who I am in the world ...

I grew up thinking my Christian identity was who I was in this world. I've since been through a series of transformations, and while I no longer resonate with that deeply rooted identity, I have not fully detached from it either. I am on a journey of finding my highest and most authentic self outside the Christian lens.

I am Ama, a Ghanaian-born child that left her country at the tender age of three to come to Canada. I am the daughter of Joe Kusi Appiah and Theresa Afi, immigrant parents who worked day and night in order to provide my siblings and me with a better life. Our home was full of laughter, love and music but also full of sadness, agony and severe discipline camouflaged by our parents' trauma. School became more of a torment than an advantage for me. I turned to dance, food and marijuana to escape from emotions and feelings too strong for me to understand. I got married, left school to run a family business to please my loved ones and make them proud, to then get divorced, lose the business and almost end my life in a car accident.

I am a soul that aspires to be a beacon of light shining bright in the darkest places. I am a mother that loves and cherishes her children and allows them to grow into their unique selves. I am a daughter that loves and accepts with no remorse, situations which have had me question my worth. I am a wife that gives, affirms and celebrates my partner and understands that my happiness is found in my own hands, creating a harmonious balance in our union.

I am a sister and friend that loves deeply and goes the extra mile, learning that I cannot be the saviour of all. I am a listening ear, a dance partner, one who encourages and a reminder of your greatness. I am a healer searching for my own healing, demonstrating to others what is possible. I am the one with the golden voice that emanates a room with words so pure and true.

This is the next story I want written for women ...

This is one of the hardest truths I've had to express. I've resisted opening up to this particular question due to the fear of being judged and sounding biased. As much as I want to be for all women today, I can't help but think about myself and other indigenous women. I can't help but think about the unfairness of history towards us. I can't help but think about how feminism is a great movement that has shifted the workforce. It does not have women like me in mind.

I can't help but think about how melanated women have been looked down upon and placed at the bottom of the list in society where we still need to work twice as hard and be twice as good to be successful. Where we are hired as a gesture of tokenisation in order to fulfil a quota. This may sound like a broken record, yet it is a truth many still experience in 2022.

So, the true story I would like written for women is a story of women of colour being given the same opportunities as their compatriots, where our skin tone or kink in our hair does not speak for us, but we are 'judged by the content of our character', as MLK said.

The story I want written for women is that black women are not seen as a threat to their less-melanated sisters, where true allyship is experienced without wanting to take away our own voices, but standing with us when we are beaten down by capitalism and Western society's white supremacy patriarchy.

The story I want to be written for women is a story that shifts the trope of the strong, angry, seductive black women into a story of soft, delicate, quintessential, joyful and sacred women that simply want to be seen for what they hold inside. A story where all women of all creeds, hues, shapes and sizes can finally stand for one another to create a quantum shift in this universe.

This is the next story I am writing for myself ...

Through persistence and courage, I have broken through barriers in my mind, and I believe in my skills and abilities. I have stepped out of my comfort zone, overcome childhood trauma and healed my inner child with patience, care and love. I am abundant and radiate this everywhere I go, I have found purpose in my authenticity, and I lend a helping hand to the needy, widowed and orphaned. My mind is the centre of divine operations! Infinite potential lives in me and I create the life I deserve. No shame, obstacle, fear, calamity, lies or betrayal keep me away from my divine path. I am a miracle, holding the universe in perfect alignment. I matter. I shine my light. I have taken back all that the lotus and cankerworm devoured. I am divine. I am like a tree planted by streams of water: I produce good fruits every season.

I am a connoisseur of wealth. I understand wealth; I walk in wealth and eat wealth. Failure is proof of my persistence as I step over every trap. My frequency is unconditional love, gratitude, joy, bliss, ease and flow. I am a creator, healer, mother, father, child, sister, brother, friend, husband and wife. I am who I am.

I am a thriving survivor, a warrior, a child of *Twereduapɔn Nyame* (the God I can lean on) with a spirit that cannot be tamed. I am the one who has lost so much but gained knowledge and understanding in the process. I am the one who has overcome obstacles and decided to spread my wings and fly, no matter how many times I fall. As queen mother Maya Angelou said, 'Still I rise.'

Sarah Rapp

30 | From: Germany | Lives: Vienna, Austria

Only if every woman (and frankly every human) has a voice at the table, will it create a safe space where every woman can write their own empowered, vivid and life-changing story.

This is who I am in the world ...

A global citizen, a human connector, a creative brain, a changemaker and a coffee-lover, this is me today, Sarah, in a nutshell. My mission is to connect the world by reducing fears about other cultures, giving everyone a voice at the table and encouraging others to embrace diversity. I live and breathe my global journey that aims to discover what it takes to be global in today's fast-paced and culturally mixed world.

I'm a global citizen at heart and don't identify with one culture or one place anymore. Having the enormous privilege to meet, work and live with people from all across the globe allows me to grow, speak up with other communities and empower others to do the same.

Growing up in Germany (that's what I call Sarah 1.0), my life looked 100% different. I was very shy and insecure, afraid to speak up or think outside the box. For the longest time in my life, I was trapped in a world I didn't belong to; a world where creativity, risk-taking and cultural diversity didn't exist. A world where one must play by the written and unwritten rules, obey things that have always been done that way and where I was afraid to speak up.

All this led to multiple nervous breakdowns, anxiety attacks and loads of therapy. The good news is that all this sparked a new version of myself: Sarah 2.0. Leaving Germany when I was twenty-five, moving to Malta, then to Vienna, exploring more than forty-five countries in-between and now working with more than 115 countries on a daily basis were the game-changers. I found myself in the diverse world out there, one piece in every single culture I was privileged to get to know.

This was exactly the moment when I started 'how to Be global', an initiative that aims to discover what it takes to be global in today's fast-paced and culturally mixed world. Today, the *how to Be global* podcast just hit ten thousand downloads with a reach in more than one hundred countries, and most importantly, gives thirty orphans in Accra, Ghana, a future with the how to Be global scholarship in collaboration with the Accra Street Academy.

Change is what I truly love and thrive on. Right at this moment, I'm embarking on the Sarah 3.0 journey, which introduces mindfulness and inner peace into the fast-paced and roller-coaster life.

This is the next story I want written for women ...

The story I next want to be written for women is their very own, empowered, vivid and life-changing story!

'One person can make a difference, and everyone should try it.' – John F Kennedy

In fact, this is my vision for any human, no matter what background, look, race and gender they identify with. I truly believe that only if we begin to write the next story as global citizens, we'll come closer and closer to the goal.

We're all living on one planet, yet humans are treated differently depending on where they are located. Too often, the values, boundaries and 'common sense' approaches to equality aren't applied in other countries, which reinforces the need to advocate strongly for equal rights and equal chances! No matter how you look, where you were born, which language you're speaking or which gender you identify yourself with, what matters is that you are human.

Only if every woman (and frankly every human) has a voice at the table, will it create a safe space where every woman can write their own empowered, vivid and life-changing story.

In travelling the world extensively and working with diverse people, I realise that racism, unhealthy boundaries and fear of the unknown are rising fast. This is alarming, given how many of today's global challenges require collective solutions and a unified sense of purpose.

Everyone can do a small part, respecting people for who they are and what they believe in, and replace stereotypes and prejudices with curiosity! That's one of the reasons why I'm a proud ambassador for the United Nations Foundation campaign #EqualEverywhere – 'We won't stop until girls and women are equal everywhere.'

This is the next story I am writing for myself...

I had just recently embarked on my Sarah 3.0 journey when I got introduced to the concept of mindfulness, stillness and taking breaks in the middle of the storm. I had no idea that this was exactly what I needed in my life. I'm constantly trying to chase the bigger, higher and greater impact not only for me, but most importantly, for the world and the people who live on it.

I'm learning that if you don't feel heard and seen: take a break. Sit still. Just *be* for a minute. You won't believe the magic that happens after you do that!

As I'm just embarking on my Sarah 3.0 journey, I'm laying the foundation for Sarah 4.0.

A version of myself that truly knows how to deal with my emotions and fears, a version of myself who is ready to take on the big stages around the world. Planting seed number one: one day, I'll have my own Netflix/TV show called *How to Be Global*, which will bring diversity and inclusion to the forefront and especially give people a voice who aren't heard (enough) at the moment!

A version of myself who will empower, inspire and educate millions of others to be brave, bold and go big to make a difference. Planting seed number two: one day, every single person will have the opportunity to join the how to Be global academy, which will result in a handover of an official global passport. I believe in a world in which it doesn't matter where you come from and which citizenship you have, the only thing that matters is that you're a responsible global citizen.

My story is full of taking action, speaking up, being mindful, and of course, being global! Let's create a global force for good!

Nettie Floyd

55 | From: Victoria, Australia | Lives: Sunshine Coast, Queensland, Australia

I want women to have the privilege of witnessing as they expand, live and trust in life and love like never before.

This is who I am in the world ...

I am love, grace, integrity, compassion, strength and kindness. I am sincere. I am a deep feeler. I am a highly intuitive mentor. I am a family pattern changer. I believe love is the magic in life.

I am a mother; it's still my favourite thing to be. I am a friend. I am a soul sister. My first experience of what unconditional love felt like was the day I became a mother.

Over the last twenty years, through formal studies and life experience, my heart-centred soul purpose work has evolved into reconnecting women with their own hearts, supporting them to heal and create a whole new version of normal. This can be done through working one on one or group work. An area I excel in is supporting women to overcome their emotional trauma and improve their self-worth.

I support them as they let go of guilt, shame and fear, allowing women to feel their trauma to heal, as it gently rises to the surface, without the fear of it consuming them. They become free and create a new way of being as they find their spark to live a full and happy life.

I have facilitated classes and workshops for human and spiritual development for the last ten years.

Like many women drawn to me, I grew up in extreme dysfunction and all types of abuse that continued off and on into my thirties. I had a core belief system that told me I was nothing and deserved nothing. I was sensitive, shy and was programmed to believe

I deserved to be abused. I felt invisible, defective, abandoned, unsafe, unworthy of love and extremely insecure. I didn't fit in, and I felt I didn't belong in this thing called life.

I remember watching and listening to older female family members when I was around thirteen, who were bitter, judgemental and harsh. This was my first experience of being grateful that I didn't 'fit in'. I made a promise to myself that day that I would do life differently. I started breaking family patterns without realising what I was doing.

I left home when I was fifteen, working full-time and living in a boarding house. I was fortunate enough to work for a family that was the opposite of my own, which gave me hope that a new way was possible. I remain grateful for this life-changing connection.

In my adult years I was so desperate to be loved that I allowed abuse and settled for scraps of conditioned love in my relationships. Ignoring the constant red flags of words and actions not matching, I often allowed in people whose inactions would eventually lead to me being reactive. I didn't want to stay in the world.

I had a nervous breakdown in my thirties, which was my biggest breakthrough. I found the courage to leave many dysfunctional relationships with a desire to find and show my children a different version of normal. In choosing to find a new way for my children, it eventually led to choosing a new way for me.

My biggest trauma in life was when, seven years into my new life with my two beautiful boys, I lost custody of my eight-year-old son. It was harder than ever to stay in the world, as being a mum was where I excelled, and this role was the absolute sunshine in my life. He is now an adult; thankfully our bond was never broken, and we have both overcome the grief of being torn apart.

Some years later, my eldest son chose not to be in my life. It took me some time to get the message, however, I came to realise that where I had gone wrong in my parenting was not making myself as important as my children. My eldest son naturally bonded closer with his father, and regardless of what I did or didn't do, being brought up solely by his father was his happy place.

I have overcome deep depression, extreme anxiety, PTSD, chronic sleep disorders and the grief of my children not being in my daily life. I spent most of my life not wanting to be here and now I'm glad that I am.

I am most passionate about the quality of relationships in my life and there has never been a truer saying than 'friends are the family we choose', as these are whom I am so grateful for. The unconditional love, support and joy we all bring to each other makes life magical.

I have always believed everything happens for a reason. At this end of my life, all I have been through and overcome has now become my soul purpose work. Heart-centred healing that empowers others to heal all areas of their lives.

This is the next story I want written for women ...

I want every woman to be free to be her true self in all areas of her life.

I want all women to be truly seen, heard, believed, validated and honoured for being them. To become free of past trauma, outdated family patterns and false core beliefs of not being enough, and to know that from love, no matter what they desire, ANYTHING IS POSSIBLE.

I want women to have the privilege of witnessing as they expand, live and trust in life and love like never before as they learn how to become their own best healer.

This is the next story I am writing for myself ...

I want to continue being an example of my life's work and for my online digital business to help thousands of women of all ages from all over the world. I want to travel, doing workshops and motivational speaking in communities, connecting women together at a heart and soul level.

I wish to create overflowing financial abundance and a foundation of financial support for women that need a hand in times of financial difficulty.

In my personal life, I will be bolder, more spontaneous and adventurous. I will allow love in and live even deeper than ever before.

I would also like to learn Latin dance.

Always from love, Nettie xxx

Rachel De Summa

36 | From: Melbourne, Australia | Lives: Warrenbayne, Australia

I found myself asking, 'What is it that will bring us into a deeper connection with ourselves, each other, and the Earth?

This is who I am in the world ...

I am a lover of nature, a community connector and an earth steward. I nurture communities and connect people with themselves, each other and the natural world. Having worked in community development spaces, youth leadership and mentoring, I ran my own business as a forest therapy guide. As an earth steward, I listen to places and ask what a place wants and needs. I observe, move slowly, act humbly and in ways that I hope will benefit the land, the beings on the land and us humans, without fully knowing the long-term impacts of my actions.

In 2017 I walked the Camino from Portugal to Spain, searching for my purpose and had a defining moment in a beautiful paddock. There were sunbeams glinting off a light hazy mist and butterflies were fluttering around me. The vegetation was glowing amongst a flurry of red flowers. I was struck by the exquisite beauty of nature at that moment. Then, immediately after my heart had been cracked open in awe, I felt a deep sense of grief that beautiful places like this are being destroyed by humans. From this intermingled love and grief arose this deep desire to protect and care for earth.

I feel a particular love and appreciation of trees and forests. I have been to protests about old growth forest logging. I visited logging coup sites near Warburton and felt the eerie silence and devastation. When I travelled across the Tarkine in Tasmania I saw the extent of this destruction driving past vast kilometres of logging operations. I felt so much grief at the sight of small spindly trees being 'harvested' by big machinery.

These mass plantations feel so wrong at a deep body level in me. This practice is not honouring life. Tree harvesting can be done differently, with respect and moderation. Use what we need and give back. I have come to realise that my pain and sadness for the suffering on the earth is so intrinsically linked to my love of life and all beings.

I began offering reiki with trees. I start with offering gratitude for the tree, its life and gifts, and then drop into my heart space and feel the tree as a living, pulsing being flowing with life. Trees want to build relationships with us. They're here waiting for us to find our way to them.

I found myself asking, 'What is it that will bring us into a deeper connection with ourselves, each other and the earth?' I wanted to share intentional ways of being in nature with others – connecting with our senses, other beings and place. Forest therapy offers a gateway for people to build their own relationship with nature, in their own way.

I live on a regenerative agriculture sheep farm with other families and adults with similar values. We are co-creating a beautiful, intentional community together. Each day I wake to bird and insect calls. The sun greets me over expansive native grass-filled paddocks. I spend my day with children, playing, listening and sharing food with families. I daydream, nap, sing with the land and allow the feelings, images and sensations that arise to flow through me. I cook and receive shared meals, and we have a rowdy dinner table where we offer gratitude and appreciation for the food and cooks. I am coming home to myself and coming home to my place in the world.

This is the next story I want written for women ...

The story I want rewritten for women is one where we are deeply and intimately connected to the wisdom of the earth and connected with each other and ourselves. I want everyone to fall in love with the earth again. Women can play such a beautiful role in that as mothers, daughters, sisters, friends, visionaries, leaders and lovers of land and place. Love moves us to care for ourselves, each other and the land. Care and love of this wild earth is so needed right now, and we all play a part in that. I want women to know their gifts, their connection to all of life and to be able to connect with the great mystery of life that links us all. As custodians of the earth, we can come together and care for Country, care for each other and care for ourselves in ways that are supportive of life.

This is the next story I am writing for myself ...

My role as an earth steward is deeply entwined in my story. The love and care I have for the earth and my pain at the destruction of the world move me to build relationships with people, build the resilience of our food system, buy food locally, share skills and learn from others about my home.

I am listening to what is next for me, what wants to emerge as my next expression for life. I have been stripping away old cultural conditioning and finding new ways to be here, at this moment. I want to bring people into connection with nature so that we can fall in love with the earth again and be moved to care for her.

I am part of a weekly nature connection program for children at the farm. I want to demonstrate that there are other ways of living, like here on this farm, and invite people into this space for healing, inspiration, connection and rejuvenation. Together with my community, we are building resilience in our food system, energy generation, social networks and building on the ecological restoration of our home.

I am so grateful to be where I am and curious to see how this grows and evolves. We practice gratitude and are custodians of this place. We each bring different aspects and gifts to our place, and this collaboration and diversity is so beautiful. I want to collaborate with others to bring forth more expressions of being in connection with earth's rhythms and living in life-giving ways.

Stephanie Hoo

39 | From: Malaysia | Lives: Bali, Indonesia

I know a time is coming when we live a life of grace and gratitude. Immersing our hearts and souls in grace is selflessly choosing to live life in the knowing that you are enough.

This is who I am in the world ...

I am Stephanie Hoo. A woman, a wife, daughter, sister and nurturing 'mother' to the many people I care for. An ambivert, a lover of nature and adventure. An old compassionate soul, kind and patient with an unwavering optimism for the positive in every situation.

My journey was ignited from a place of devastation and loss. My mother had just lost her battle with cancer. At that moment, life changed forever. I made a simple promise to myself with no understanding of exactly how it would impact my existence. I promised to dedicate my life and energy to the health and wellbeing of others. My goal was to be a guide that helped ease the pain and sadness that many deal with. I committed myself to a meaningful journey of hope and service.

There was no way of knowing where this decision would lead me, yet I sensed intuitively that the path of holistic health and wellness would become my gift to others; and so began years of ongoing passionate study. Studies that allow me to travel the world, learning from masters. Their wisdom, combined with my ever-growing knowledge, has graced me with a rare insight and understanding of the workings of the mind, body and soul.

The simple decision to change, grow, learn and be of service led to qualifications in clinical and metaphysical aromatherapy, applied metaphysics, clinical biotherapy, qi gong trainer, integrative nutrition health coach, plant-based nutrition in raw food mastery and lifestyle medicine coach. I developed a deep and profound understanding of our body's inherent intelligence to heal. The greatest test of these learnings was to heal myself from a condition that defied the conventional medical route.

Now I live in a conscious, compassionate state of understanding, allowing me the gift of guiding clients back to health and happiness. I often find myself being my client's last resort – when everyone else has given up, we begin. I have guided clients to reverse chronic lifelong conditions, assisting them to take control, make changes and fulfil their health and wellness vision.

I feel blessed to have witnessed real-life impact and results and know that my daily actions continue to fulfil that single promise I made to myself years ago. I carry my beloved mother's unfading strength and fearless courage knowing that I have a higher purpose to serve. My brand, A Gracious Life, is a tribute to her legacy – her name was Grace.

This is the next story I want written for women ...

I want riches for all women, but I humbly expect little, knowing that every woman has her journey to travel, her destiny to arrive at.

I see a future where all women become a sisterhood of support, free to be the author of their own stories, safe from judgement and acknowledged by others who have dared to dream. A future where women are gracious enough to celebrate humbly, strong enough to own their mistakes. A future that allows our imperfections to become compassion, where all are equal, free to experience the gifts of life.

I see a future where women stand together. Faithfully following our inner wisdom, listening to the voice within that inspires us to be brave and to say no to what no longer serves us. A future where women encourage each other, delivering all to our unique truths, to the healing we so desire, to the courage and acceptance to know and love ourselves for who we are. A future where action and sacrifice inspire the next generation of leaders – young women and men all over the world who look to us for strength, guidance and compassion.

I know a time is coming when we live a life of grace and gratitude. Immersing our hearts and souls in grace is selflessly choosing to live life in the knowing that you are enough. Welcoming every day with gratitude displays a divine understanding that this beautiful state is the place where humanity functions at its best.

I know there is a future where we stand united in the glorious glow of self, supported and supporting, giving and receiving, growing together for the good of all.

This is the next story I am writing for myself …

Through the humbling experiences as a caregiver for my mother, I learned the greatest of life's many lessons … I learned the precious gift of giving. It took many years to understand the full power of this concept, but slowly and surely, the gift of giving revealed itself.

In giving, I receive.

The gift of giving has continually grown over the years, taking shape in numerous unexpected ways. I never believed I would create and publish a photography book, *Life's Classroom,* where profits were donated to a foundation supporting children's formal and informal education, but I did. I never imagined that I would be the initiator to build a school for three hundred children in the slums of Nairobi, but I did. Nor did I ever imagine that I would produce a film about the Dayak communities' connection with their rainforest – a film that supported indigenous communities and their customary school, but I did. By giving, I have experienced pure and unconditional happiness without expectation. I now know that if I – WE – focus on giving, the world will receive more.

The story I want to write next for myself is simple. I am going to be part of endless transformational healing, and I am going to be the conduit that selflessly serves others who desire this life-changing experience. I will continue to self-explore, understanding and knowing the many parts of myself to better serve those I guide. I will continue to allow myself to be imperfectly perfect and be at peace, not knowing all the answers because I know that is a necessary part of my journey. I will continue to find the good in the bad, and explore the bad in the good; fully accepting that it is an amazing privilege to embody both my light and shadow self. I will continue to inspire my mind with wisdom and infuse my body with love as I discover the middle path, journeying and flowing with ease, living a gracious life.

Finally, I will continue to give.

Suzana Mihajlovic

49 | From: Melbourne, Australia | Lives: Melbourne, Australia

I see every woman being free. Free to be herself - to laugh and to cry. In this story every girl is free to play ... play from the freedom of her heart.

This is who I am in the world ...

I was born to Serbian parents who had migrated to Australia only two years before I came into the world. One of my earliest childhood memories was of the pain and trauma that migrants feel arriving in a foreign land. My deep sadness was not due to my own experience but that of my grandparents, parents and brother. In some ways they were ripped out of their homeland, from their extended family, the only community they had ever known and moved to a foreign land where they did not know the language, the strange customs or the way of life.

I also have many wonderful childhood memories, and I could not thank my parents enough for the sacrifice they made. Australia is now our home and the place that we belong.

Being a highly sensitive child, I felt people's hurt very deeply. This was both a curse and a gift. It was a very heavy burden to carry as a child. The flip side of my childhood burden was that I had a unique way of connecting to other people's souls. I somehow understood who they were on that deep level; I was able to connect and speak with their soul.

The child I was has led me to who I am in the world today. I am a lover, a partner, a best friend, a daughter, a sister, a proud aunt and godmother … In business, I am a leader and a stranger to many whom I may represent something or someone that is related to their own experience of life.

The only role that I have not experienced yet and always yearned to experience is that of being a mother. Not being able to conceive a child has left me with a deep sadness.

To me, the fundamental question is, *How do I show up in life?* From the most intimate people in my life to the stranger I meet at the grocery store. The quality of each of these relationships is ultimately impacted by whether I am living from spirit or my past conditioning. It was the spirit in that child that helped her deeply empathise with her family and other people. And that same spirit that guides me as an adult when I am not consumed by the 'monkey mind' chatter of my past.

This is the next story I want written for women ...

When I think back to that child, even in her pain, she played. She was deeply loving and gentle yet fiercely passionate and wild. She played; she was free. She loved people, yet when alone, and painfully lonely at times, she played. She was a combination of tomboy and pretty princess playing with dolls. Life was an adventure for her in this freedom, in this play.

She was cheeky yet innocent. She was a famous pop star, gymnast, teacher and a champion karate star. She laughed until her belly ached. She cried until her sobs were out of control. She was often very sad and lonely … but even through the darkest times, she faced her fears. Her body trembled when the bullies in her street would attack her … and even in her body trembling she continued forward on her path to wherever she had been going at that time.

Her father taught her to dream big. Even though she felt it impossible at the time, her father subconsciously taught her that no dream was too big for her. There was never an inkling of her not being able to achieve something because she was a woman. Gender did not ever come into the picture. Her father saw her talent and he knew deep inside that she could fulfil any dream.

This is the story I want written for women. In this story, I see every woman being free. Free to be herself – to laugh and to cry. In this story every girl is free to play … play from the freedom of her heart. Every girl is free to dream as big as her free heart desires. The girl is so important to the woman's story because it is the girl that is creating the woman.

In this story, the woman who hasn't had the freedom as a child is finally liberated. She is able to love, to dance with life, to cry. Her spirit is fierce, her soul is set alight, and it encompasses her entire being … she is connected, she is respected and when she walks in her quiet confidence, the ground beneath her rumbles. Mother earth knows her power. This is the power of the woman who is set free, this is the power and essence of every woman who has walked the earth.

From this incredible and immense power, she is able to lift other women, children and men up. When we liberate ourselves, we allow all others to be liberated in our presence.

In this story, every woman has woken up to this incredible internal power, and from this eruption, the entire planet earth is healed. Women awoken heal the societal trauma. And I believe the great awakening is here for us all, Mother Earth is calling us from deep within her womb. It is not an impossible ideology but one that is arising as we speak.

This is the next story I am writing for myself …

That migrant child came to this earth to help heal souls. I hope to fulfil my soul's purpose to the best of my capacity. I feel that I have a long way to go, that I have only just scratched the surface in fulfilling my purpose.

What I hope to add to this story is the fulfilment of the void that a motherless mother's heart has. Never in my wildest dreams did I ever believe that I would not have children of my own. What purpose does life really have without a family?

I do know however, that God always fills a void. By staying in trust and keeping the faith, motherhood will be something that I will experience.

As I write, a voice speaks to my heart. It whispers, *Well, why can't life be your child, Suzana?* I will have to contemplate this question.

Isotta Rossoni

32 | From: Sydney, Australia | Lives: Between Italy and Malta

Part of my journey within, has involved coming to terms with the fact that despite sex generally being a source of fun and joy, it can also engender negative experiences.

This is who I am in the world ...

I was born a traveller. When I was one year old, huddled up in my mother's arms, I boarded my first intercontinental flight. Since then, I have embarked on numerous journeys around the world.

Nothing gives me more of a kick than scratching countries off my scratch map! It's taken me a while to realise that the most exhilarating and profoundly challenging journey of all has been the journey within, the process of getting to know the unique and most vulnerable sides of myself. I was a very insecure teen. I felt endlessly lost, like I didn't truly belong. My family has a history of emigration. I, too, emigrated when I was young, and this contributed to my muddled sense of identity. The need to belong has a long history in social psychology – human beings crave to feel part of something bigger, a group, a community. Yet our societies teach us that belonging ought to take on predefined forms, that we should belong to an ethnic group, a religious community, the nation. I tried very hard to squeeze into these boxes and failed.

When I moved to London at nineteen, I was eager to leave all pressures and categories behind. I sought anonymity. I wanted to get lost in the crowd. And I did – lose myself – but I also found myself. Over the years, my studies, my work as a criminologist focusing on sexual and gender-based violence in migration and the people I met along the way, have helped me realise that I am privileged enough to consider myself a citizen of the world. I possess the 'right' passports and a favourable enough socioeconomic status to open all doors. I am also a woman who's curious about getting to know her body, exploring pleasure and sexuality. Yet despite being white and Western, I still grapple with the challenges attached to womanhood.

Part of my journey within, which was made substantially easier by the insights gleaned from my profession, has involved coming to terms with the fact that despite sex generally being a source of fun and joy, it can also engender negative experiences. In fact, even some of my sexual encounters weren't fully consensual. This awareness and the conversations I have had with many women in the past few years have led me to realise that I am part of a broader community of women facing similar and concurrently unique trials. I am a runner, a ballet dancer, a feminist. Forever on a journey and at peace with my identity being intersectional and in constant evolution.

This is the next story I want written for women ...

The story I want next written for women is one where the stigma that surrounds sex is lifted, where women can talk freely about the good and the bad of sex without shame or fear of judgement. Our societies represent sex and violence in highly sensationalistic terms. In doing so, they obscure a host of day-to-day realities, leading us to becoming oblivious to 'ordinary', almost routine forms of violence in our sexual encounters. Ultimately, sex is about communication. It centres on communicating – verbally and non-verbally – what we want, what we like and what we don't. It's also about truly tuning in to listen to what others are trying to express. Like so many other women – and men – I was never taught that asking and listening to ourselves and others lies at the heart of sex. I was never told that I have a right to say no if I didn't feel like engaging in a sexual act. I was never made to realise that my desires, especially in this context, matter. Or that, indeed, other people's desires matter too; that good and healthy sex involves being receptive to one's wishes, respecting the other's desires and learning how to communicate. I heard the word 'consent' many years after my first sexual encounter. I dream of a world where children learn about consent much earlier on in life. For this to happen, safe spaces need to be created for women and men to engage in respectful and constructive dialogue around consent, what it looks like to them, what they find easy, difficult, unacceptable, exciting. In general, we should all have more down-to-earth conversations about sex in the settings that feel appropriate to us. We should all work to make our world one where women can enjoy sex without the guilt and shame that has long been imposed on them by our patriarchal societies, and most of all, without unnecessary and unwarranted suffering.

This is the next story I am writing for myself …

A long time has passed since I packed my bags and escaped to London. I have become more outspoken, less apologetic, more confident – but that insecure teen is still part of who I am … and it's totally okay. Just as I aspire for a world where we can talk about sex in a healthy and truly genuine manner, I also hope that my journey within will help me gradually accept the aspects of my being that I would much rather lock away in the depths of my soul. They will most likely always make me feel uncomfortable, but luckily I am no longer afraid of feeling the uneasiness that for a long time weighed me down. I have a visceral need to make myself useful, which has influenced my life and career choices in distinct ways.

The story I would like to write for myself is one where I can capitalise on this need to contribute to making a difference. My goal is to join forces with like-minded individuals to set up an NGO at the intersections of sexual health, empowerment and sexual and gender-based violence. An NGO that serves less to glorify my achievements and acts more as a space for free, intersectional dialogue around sex. A space where no-one feels that they need to make excuses for who they are or what they want.

Toni Lontis

55 | Lives: Tallebudgera Valley, Gold Coast, QLD, Australia on the land of the Yugambah people.

Whenever a woman speaks up, just believe her and what she has to say.

This is who I am in the world ...

I live with my husband, our small dog Tiki, and up until recently, seven beautiful little goats and two magnificent llamas. I like to think of myself as a soul living the human experience and intuitively following my purpose.

I am the product of a millennia of maternal line epigenetics and intergenerational trauma, which contributed to family dysfunction. I was born with a congenital facial defect which resulted in ongoing and dangerous infections and ultimately led to permanent left-side facial palsy. I could not smile properly, close my left eye, raise my left eyebrow. As you can imagine, school was less than ideal, and I suffered at the hands of my classmates and teachers. My inability to smile greatly impacted my capacity to build social connection from infancy onwards.

My low self-esteem and worthlessness continued into adulthood, where I made really bad choices that led to sexual assault, sexual abuse, domestic violence and abusive relationships. I refused to accept help, which ultimately led to a complete physical and mental breakdown in my forties. My wonderfully supportive GP suggested that if I didn't take medication, stop working in a high-level stressful role and heal/deal with my pain and trauma, I would not make it to fifty! Thus began my self-discovery and healing journey, which, ten years later, led to the publication of my book, *Resilience – Memoir of a broken little girl discovering a woman of strength and beauty*.

The book took me to places that I could not have anticipated. My decision to say yes to all things that terrified me, to follow my intuition and trust the universe, led to the creation of a global broadcasting empire. I now help people to find their voice and share their messages with the world, showcasing the uniqueness of each human being and their businesses, brands, companies and stories.

This is the next story I want written for women ...

'We are the granddaughters of the witches you weren't able to burn.' – Tish Thawer

Firstly, whenever a woman speaks up, just believe her and what she has to say.

For generations, women have felt a fear of speaking out, because historically it is tied to a fear for our survival. It's ingrained in my DNA to be a good girl – 'don't create waves', 'don't speak out', don't put myself in a position where I'm open to judgement, don't step out of the intergenerational plan. It takes courage and healing to raise your voice!

I believe that the future will be paved with powerful women operating at a higher level of consciousness and in positions where they impact decisions. However, I still see the impact of the way that we shame women in society who stand tall in these positions, still we see disproportionate criticism of women in political and leadership roles.

It takes more than saying that we support other women, we have a responsibility to actively challenge and confront our own judgements, biases and unconscious patriarchal beliefs and call these out, so that we do not bring women down. This includes noticing the times where we side with men against other women. Even if we don't agree with women, we can still wholeheartedly support them and encourage their right to be in a position where they can be seen and heard.

Women are wondrous beings, marvellous creators. After all, we create new human beings from a few cells without so much as a conscious thought. I want all women to embrace the wonder of being female, either by birth or by choice. To understand the power of feminine energy as the creative power that has and will solve the issues that we face as a planet and a human race.

Feminine energy is nurturing and compassionate, kind and empathetic, patient and emotional, and magnificently intuitive. Empowered and balanced feminine energy is being authentic, receiving and vulnerable, and in its unbalanced form presents as insecure, co-dependent, needy, overemotional, lacking in boundaries and manipulative.

It is becoming more urgent for women to cultivate their feminine energy and encourage the men in their lives to cultivate and balance their masculine and feminine energy. Unfortunately, our culture values the masculine energy of doing over the feminine energy of creating. I want women to reflect, be creative, ground themselves in nature, be spontaneous and playful, expressive, boost their emotional intelligence, and above all, tune into their intuition as the guidance of their soul.

The next decade is a powerful one for women, particularly those over the age of thirty-five. This is our time to lead the next generation of women into the rebalancing of masculine and feminine, the end of patriarchy as we have known it. This is a unique time to be alive and follow in our soul's purpose because it will take many, many women to shift the energy and rebalance the earth. This is our destiny, our legacy.

This is the next story I am writing for myself ...

I want my soon-to-be-born granddaughter to grow up in a world where she can think and do whatever she dreams of.

My role in changing the world so that it is more aligned with this is by showing up as my imperfect self, by daring to believe in myself and creating the right mindset with education and action taking.

Everyone has a story, everyone has something to say and wisdom to share, and I want to inspire, empower, educate and help the world one show at a time. I am a broadcaster with my own channel, Toni TV, and my own streaming TV network, The Everyday Women's Network. I truly believe that the foundations of change are in giving women a strong voice using non-traditional media platforms.

There is nothing more powerful than when a woman harnesses both her righteous anger and the nurturing wisdom that heals both herself and others, and my role is to hand her the mic and broadcast it to the world.

Catherine Shovlin

59 | From: Newcastle, England | Lives: Between Bali and London

A world beyond equality where all women feel entitled, allowed, supported and valued exactly as they are. Not only the most courageous or audacious or privileged women. Not only the gold medallists and the CEOs, but women everywhere.

This is who I am in the world ...

It was snowy outside, somewhere in rural Netherlands, about ten years ago. I'd jumped out of my comfort zone to join ALIA – a leadership event with decidedly more leanings towards the esoteric than I was used to. I wasn't sure why I had been called to this event since I felt I had everything very well-organised. Successful business, entertaining children, nice house, cool projects, interesting travel. All the boxes were ticked.

I looked intently into my partner's eyes, looking for the life purpose we were supposed to be identifying. Letting my thinking brain step away for a moment as I breathed into my heart. A very clear image came to me of a drill driving a hole through a brick wall. It didn't seem to make much sense, but I shared it anyway.

'Breaking through walls!' he exclaimed. 'It's exactly what you do.'

I wasn't sure. It sounded unpleasant. Painful, even.

'Actually, once I identify them, they usually just melt away,' I said, thinking out loud. 'Then they're easy to walk through. I wonder if we make most of them up? Maybe my grandmother was right and there's no such word as can't. We just need to melt down a wall or two that's blocking our view.'

I identified *walking through walls* as my life purpose on that day, though I soon realised I'd always been living by it. Walking through the gender wall in my twenties to work in the oil and gas industry – and probably being the first director to breastfeed in a board meeting (well, they do tend to go on too long and a baby has to be fed). Through the corporate wall of protection into starting my own business – despite being sole provider for three children under six. Through that high wall surrounding the refugee camp to bring moments of colour, peace and joy to their challenging world.

I've been lucky enough (or manifested enough) to have experienced great diversity living in a European capital, in the South American Andes, the African desert and now the jungle in Asia. Working in big businesses, startups and NGOs, with board members, artists, disenfranchised teenagers, dementia patients, refugees and villagers. Learning wisdom from every single person I've met along the way, gathering perspectives and broadening my own.

This is the next story I want written for women …

I was running a circle for fourteen-year-old girls – a mix of Syrians and locals in the small mountain village in Northern Lebanon where the informal refugee camp had developed.

'All our lives we've been told to be careful. To be afraid. That there's danger outside the walls of the house. So we think that's true.'

'They don't tell our brothers to be afraid.'

'How can we do the same things they do when we feel we're in danger all the time? We want to be brave. To have adventures.'

So many times, I hear a version of this story. It shifts in different cultures, different situations, but the subliminal programming is still hypnotising us. Even where we have equal rights, equal pay, equal opportunities – we can feel the disadvantage. Because we don't quite believe it in our bones.

There are echoes in my own life, despite all my advantages of education, political and social freedom, choices. Forcing myself to be equal to men worked for me, but it took so much of my energy and peace of mind.

I didn't see the walls that society had built and I was respecting. Walls for women of shame and decorum, desirability and keeping the peace. And the walls I built inside myself – I don't know enough, not old enough, not young enough, not creative enough … simply *not enough*.

Now it's time for me, for all of us, to see those walls clearly. And let them dissolve so we can walk through them.

The next story I want written for women is of a world beyond equality. A world where all women feel entitled, allowed, supported and valued exactly as they are. Not only the most courageous or audacious or privileged women. Not only the gold medallists and the CEOs, but women everywhere. I am looking to a world where all women and girls are free to choose, are comfortable in their choosing and are walking through walls without harming a hair on their head.

This is the next story I am writing for myself ...

The first part of my life was full of drive. Whatever I decided was my next goal, I found a way to realise it. My business partner had long dreamed of doing art projects in a refugee camp but had always been thwarted. 'Telling Catherine was like throwing a dog a bone,' he joked, 'she was going to get it to happen no matter what.'

More recently I walked through the walls of ambition, acquisition and certainty. I resigned from jobs, got rid of 70% of my possessions. Cleared space with no expectations. No plan.

My guides and teachers tell me, 'You've done the hard work. In this life and other lifetimes. Now you can do your best work by relaxing, meditating, playing, enjoying.'

Sounds fantastic, right? Yet it's strange how hard it is to stick to after a lifetime of doing the opposite. I'm a work in progress. Resisting the knee-jerk reaction to DO something. Anything. To fill in the blanks. Silencing the voices in my head that interrupt my moments of peace with accusations of laziness or pointlessness. Breathing more slowly. Walking more slowly. Reacting more slowly.

I love my life now, using my training in shamanic healing and as an end-of-life doula to walk through the wall between life and death, physical and spirit.

I don't always remember. Old habits die hard. My stress response is to revert to my old ways, to hide in busyness. But I have all of the second half of my life to un-work on it. To spread change in the world by learning to be me. To forgive myself, accept myself, allow myself to be exactly who I am. And like magic, without walls, that spreads to everyone else.

Kim Bleeze

50 | From: Australia | Lives: Gypsy, destination unknown.

Know yourself, recognize your intuition, psychic nature and spirit-speaking abilities you were born with, yet may have forgotten over a lifetime of someone else telling you who to be.

This is who I am in the world ...

I wear many hats: mother, publisher, medium, psychic, speaker, teacher, author, visionary and creative. I am an advocate and teacher for spiritual truth and believe in the importance of living in alignment with our souls' path and our essential connection to the spirit world.

My most significant accomplishments to date? Teaching others to embrace their abilities to communicate with the unseen world and founding *Fierce Truths Spiritual Magazine* and the *BE Fierce: Soul Truth and Spirituality* app.

I am an earth-honouring, no-shoes kind of girl with a gypsy heart that loves to laugh, beat her drum to the morning sun (or any time of the day, really), dance under the light of the full moon and have naked swims alone any chance she gets.

I live on my terms, independently from societal norms. I've always felt separate from the world, like I'm a stranger here, one that doesn't quite fit in. Whereas once that bothered me and made me feel invisible and small, I'm now proud of my naturalness to stand out from the crowd and think differently.

I stand for love, acceptance and the empowerment that comes from understanding ourselves from a higher level of consciousness, from seeing the 'bigger cosmic picture'. I see soul lessons where others see failures and mistakes, and I'm open to meeting my fears head-on (mostly) and my work with spirit as a medium lights me up the most.

I am a woman who is constantly changing and evolving. I'm not afraid of digging into the core of who I am to bring out the best I can be – I don't always get it right, and I'm happy to own that part of me. As my work slowly moves towards the shamanic plant medicine path, I'm transitioning between who I was and who I am becoming, and sometimes, I still feel lost in that in-between space. So I'm deeply in the process of allowing myself to be divinely guided toward the next steps on my path.

I've allowed myself to change, grow, heal and evolve in ways I'm still trying to comprehend and articulate. I've spent what felt like lifetimes (probably has been) weaving in and out of bad situations that brought me pain and heartache. Childhood sexual trauma, rape, intravenous drug abuse to numb my pain, years of heart-wrenching domestic violence because I didn't believe I deserved better, debilitating worthlessness and inadequacies around choosing healthy intimate relationships. My capacity for self-love was non-existent, and the lack of it turned my life into one of self-abuse and self-sabotage. I spent years hurting myself or allowing others to hurt me instead.

Realising I was psychic and discovering spirit changed everything. I no longer felt alone in the world or separate. I could communicate with the unseen world; realising that was a pretty big deal for me. It gave my life substance and meaning and faith that I had a higher purpose here, that the life I had led to date hadn't been a waste, and I wasn't a waste of space.

It took me a long time to heal and get to where I am in learning to love and accept ALL of myself and recognising my value, and it is still a journey that continues now – well, I certainly give it a good crack, anyway.

This is the next story I want written for women ...

Know yourself, recognise your intuition, psychic nature and spirit-speaking abilities you were born with yet may have forgotten over a lifetime of someone else telling you who to be. Awaken to your amazingness and true value to the world.

Whether raising a family or speaking to millions, you have the same worth and right to be here and shine your light. Allow yourself to express yourself fully without fear and away from shame. So, STOP fitting yourself into a tiny box of someone else's creation.

You've hidden in that darkness for too long, unable to recognise your shadow for what it is, a valuable part of you as worthy of your acceptance and love as your light is.

Don't care what the world thinks of you; it only matters what you feel about yourself, even when you f*ck up. Honour all of yourself – the good, bad and ugly – and stop judging yourself. Regardless of what the past version of you has endured, you're not that woman anymore. So, see the lessons it taught you as gifts to help you grow. Especially the significant experiences targeted at your heart; they are the ones that will help you discover yourself the most and teach you things about yourself that no-one else can.

Then, lean into the limitless capacity of love already inside you and manifest the life you desire from there. It's time to stop feeling invisible to the world; it's time to be seen; it's time to be heard.

This is the next story I am writing for myself ...

The woman I've always envisioned myself becoming is that woman who lives her life to the fullest, that says 'F*CK YES' to life and herself unbounded by fears or self-doubts. To get to the end of my life knowing with certainty that I have no regrets because I've left nothing out I've wanted to do.

So, I check myself and reflect on whether or not I feel I am living that truth. Sometimes my answer is yes. Sometimes it's no. I pause, recalibrate and ask myself what I can do better. So, the story I now write for myself is this …

To align deeply with the woman that says yes to life. To walk my talk and truth unwaveringly and without challenge from my ego telling me I can't. To always allow me to grow, learn and deepen into my divine nature and the unseen world. To believe wholeheartedly that I am enough, and then, from that place of self-love and acceptance, build a publishing and media empire that instils global change and spiritual growth from within – teaching each person we touch to embrace their capacity to love themselves and honour their journey because we have the right to shine our light brightly.

Maria Boulatsakos

33 | From: New South Wales, Australia | Lives: New South Wales, Australia

I will continue to be brave and proceed with gratitude. I need to gently move with the ebbs and flows of life. I have a deep understanding that my decisions may come with challenges but also great reward and opportunity.

This is who I am in the world ...

I am a daughter, sister, wife, carer and friend who loves taking photos of lasting memories.

I am a huge empath and your biggest cheerleader. I believe equity is not justice and everyone deserves the chance to succeed. I am from a working-class migrant family and have been blessed with enough. This mindset has guided my life choices such as volunteering in underprivileged communities and for charities. I appreciate what I have because of what I have witnessed. I am very family orientated and am currently navigating with my mother on how to best care for my father who has early onset Alzheimer's disease. Some days are tougher than others, but I believe we are given no more than we can handle.

I am a fur mum to two beautiful dogs who teach me unconditional love. I am a mother figure to many, but not a mother yet. I have silently suffered unexplained infertility and had severe stage four endometriosis removed. This was only by taking radical responsibility and having courageous conversations for further investigation.

I love activities that enhance my health and wellbeing. Growing up, I was a sickly and highly strung child, who, in her twenties, carried a tissue in fear of sickness. I functioned on little sleep and developed debilitating digestive issues due to stress. My nervous system was overloaded. This, however, sustained my curiosity to learn how to optimise wellness. I followed this passion into my lifelong vocation of becoming a teacher. Yet, I am a former educator after just over a decade of service. I withdrew myself from a broken system which undervalued my drive and dedication. I finally said no to burnout, fatigue and weariness and yes to me and my personal growth. I am unsure if I will return, but they do say when you know better, you do better.

With immense joy and gratitude, I am now a child and adult yoga teacher, and I host wellness workshops. The practice of yoga is my saving grace; it has brought relief to my anxiety and helped manage attachment issues, intrusive thoughts and worry. I have become a fierce advocate for self-care and self-love and have recognised the value of rest, space and a slower pace. I now can surrender and value that everything happens *for* me and not just *to* me. I welcome the opportunity and time to heal. Some may call me a spiritual seeker striving to understand my soul's purpose.

This personal work has guided my acceptance of life and death. I am hopeful for a peaceful afterlife and appreciate that we all die an earthly death but our spirit is never lost, and until that time, we must live each day anew and in awe. I aspire to live humbly, leaving a kind imprint on the planet. This lens has been shaped by the experience of unpredictable loss and grief. I have witnessed the spectrum of interpersonal struggles from trauma of inexplicable and explained illness to suicide. Not long ago, I attended my fortieth funeral service. These spanned from immediate to extended family and friends. So, I stopped counting, ceased holding my breath and agonising over death and just live one day at a time.

This is the next story I want written for women ...

I give you permission to have faith, follow your dreams and make your own success, but with boundaries. Be patient, take it slow – you don't have to do it all. Society's construct on women and our own limitations is not tangible or achievable. Being a high-functioning overachiever and people pleaser never allowed me to have 'me time'. I treaded water in this rat-race for years, crossing off the never-ending checklist. Just be you and do what you want – it is not sustainable to make everyone else happy, just don't burn your bridges. Your priority is your own happiness, wellbeing and health. You deserve to rest, integrate and self-care. Find your thing that brings you joy and revel in this.

To the young girls, shine bright – you are unique, so love your own body, ideas and beliefs. In this world you can be compassionate, kind and conscious and still be vulnerable, strong and resilient. It is inevitable that we will upset and disappoint others. But you don't have to be more for anyone else. You are worthy, so choose you!

Finally, we are always learning on the journey. Let knowledge give you opportunities to seek more and inspire others. Listen to your intuition, don't let external factors cloud your judgement. Ask the hard questions, get that second opinion and keep your spirit and passion alive. Find your tribe. You will thrive and flourish with a support network that sees, holds and lifts you with their tools and wisdom. Create a community so you can problem-solve and celebrate together.

This is the next story I am writing for myself ...

I will continue to be brave and proceed with gratitude. I need to gently move with the ebbs and flows of life. I have a deep understanding that my decisions may come with challenges but also great reward and opportunity. Timing is just an illusion, I must pause and breathe, and remember *I have time* and embrace the imperfections of my journey. I will remind myself I am worthy of love, personal success and being a mother when the time is right. I can continue to thrive by acknowledging that deep rest restores me and helps to block out the noise to hear the deep knowing. I want to continue inspiring young people and be a beacon of hope and light through joy and pain. I do not have to live up to expectations, and I am abundant without the construct of money as I already have all that I need. I can create this new reality by unlearning the limiting beliefs that hold me back and doing things that I love and bring me joy. I say yes to what I really want and no to the things that don't serve me anymore. I will no longer sweat the small stuff, and will continue to trust and believe that everything will be how it is supposed to be as the universe works in mysterious ways.

Marcelle Rouchon

51 | From: Anse-A-Foleur, Haiti | Lives: Miami, Florida, US

The woman that I become is filled with the resiliency of Haiti, my birthplace and the courage of Anacaona, its warrior queen.

This is who I am in the world ...

I am a woman of faith – a child of God. I come from the 'Most High King', and for that reason, I know and embrace my purpose in this world.

I did not always know my spiritual identity, let alone my earthly mission. It took me a long mental journey before I understood and grasped the path that the universe has presented before me.

My name is Marcelle Rouchon. I have been happily married to Robert for almost thirty years and am a proud mom to my son Phillip, twenty-three, and daughter Kiana, twenty-eight. I'm yearning to be a grandmother as we are awaiting the birth of Kiana and her husband Emmanuel's firstborn.

To reach this point of self-love and self-identity, I went through a life-altering furnace. I emerged golden through the inner strength with which I was gifted. I have experienced sexual trauma in my teen years, and as a result it took me an eternity and tremendous efforts to accept who I am. I have learned in a labour-like pain to process my brokenness and to become whole again. Sexual trauma had stolen my innocence, which is one of the most precious gifts from the universe. My combat to reclaim and regain myself has been horrendous. The inner rage, self-doubt, guilt, shame, hopelessness, helplessness and sadness amounted to a colossal mountain for a young child to climb alone. Nonetheless, I clambered that steep and treacherous hill and was successfully reborn as a stronger and more resilient woman.

The moment I realised my true worth as a human being and my value as a woman, the road to be healed became attainable. I arose like a phoenix from its ash with a new vision and a renewed sense of purpose. Therefore, I decided to avidly lend my voice to advocate for those whose hearts have been shattered. The woman that I became is filled with the resiliency of Haiti, my birthplace and the courage of Anacaona, its warrior queen. As a survivor, I became cognisant of my calling that is to use my sordid experience to help, strengthen and inspire others.

I am the change that I seek; therefore, I dedicate my life to foster such a transformation in the lives of my community members. I have been involved in many mentorship initiatives where I have worked with young adults. My unquenchable thirst to help did not stop there. I have reached out to a wonderful organisation, Word and Action, Inc. (W&A) that is aiming to reduce the occurrence of child sexual abuse in our community. I volunteered to become a W&A ambassador and later I held the position of interim executive director. My unwavering dedication has landed me in the Florida State Senate arena. Hence, between 2017-2018, I was named vice co-chair and board member of the State Senate District 38 Health Task Force. I had the opportunity to visit the Florida State Legislature. I was able to speak with state legislators on behalf of silently suffering young girls and boys in my community.

One of my greatest honours was the opportunity that I was given to exchange with many young men and women in my community. I was able to empower them in their own brokenness and prevent them from succumbing under the weight of loneliness and hopelessness. Because of my devotion and dedication to the youths, I was often called 'community mom'. I am happy to have facilitated those gentle yet fragile souls to give themselves permission to find their voice and express their thoughts and feelings without fear. I have been in their shoes; hence, I could easily relate to them. It was important for me to reassure them that they were not alone on their rocky journey. One of the most painful realities when dealing with such a trauma is the inability to find someone you can securely and confidently share your fear and despair with. I went through my painful journey alone, without that someone. Today, I make myself available to those in need of an ear or a shoulder.

This is the next story I want written for women ...

I would not wish to rewrite a story for women. I would rather add to their story, and perhaps my humble contribution could empower more of us. In that light, I want women to find their inner core to speak up even when their voice shakes. Some topics may be harder than others to echo; however, remaining silent or in the shadows should never be part of the equation. Sadly, the glass ceiling has not been totally broken, and in many societies, it has even been reinforced.

Nonetheless, the fatality would be collective should the voice of the undermining and hurting women not be heard. They must stand their ground with dignity and pride even when their opinions may generate uneasiness among the status quo. Women must close their eyes and speak their truths until the world can no longer ignore or deny them. Lastly, I want women to know that we are much stronger when we empower one another.

This is the next story I am writing for myself ...

My next story might be entitled *From Brokenness to Beauty*. We all possess the ability to mend our broken vessel and turn it into a chef-d'oeuvre. The challenge is often to find the courage to put the pieces together. This is where support from friends, families, community members and even professionals could play a major role. Such a belief propelled me to create a non-profit organisation, Healing Xchange, Inc., which will soon be launched. Through that organisation, I hope to create a portal where victims of childhood sexual trauma and human trafficking can safely share their stories. To birth this community organisation, I was inspired by a Bible verse, Isaiah 53:5 that stipulated: 'By His stripes, we are healed.'

I was a victim of childhood sexual abuse, but today I am an advocate who is fighting to keep children safe from sexual predators. Like many young kids, my little mind could not comprehend that I did nothing wrong and that I was not 'dirty'. It took a lot of inner strength and professional support to overcome my trauma. That's why I want Healing Xchange to be a safe space for survivors to achieve similar milestones while sharing their stories and helping others. To that end, my story has just begun.

Cate Dubois

57 | From: Australia | Lives: Canggu, Bali

Who am I? I am a woman with deep intuition and a fierce fire burning to wake women of the world up to the knowing and remembrance of who they are.

This is who I am in the world ...

I've been in a role of seer, advisor and mediator since I was young, only I never took my role seriously or recognised it as my dharma, until now. I always have been extremely open to people coming to me with their thoughts, feelings and broken dreams, seeking counsel. I look through the eyes of beauty, and through those eyes, I see beauty in everyone. It is hard for me to see the flaws they see. I cannot be swayed by others' opinions of themselves or others. How arrogant to think we can improve on nature and her gifts. I believe no-one is broken, just a little – or a lot – lost at times.

I was fortunate at a young age to understand I did not think and experience life like everyone else, seeing only perfection in everything. I saw things in other people and situations many could not see. Somehow, I knew this gave me an advantage.

When I was seven years old, my best friend, Melinda, died of leukaemia. I intuitively knew she decided not to be in this world. Her world was one of sadness, her family confused, she was a girl in pain. I realised, then, we get to choose it all. On the day of her funeral, I found a gold pendant with Mother Mary carved on it. I knew, as Melinda did, everything was going to be alright. This was my kundalini awakening and early awareness that we have our own choices, inspiring a deeper knowing of myself and others.

We are here on karmic cycles, and I want to educate people about who they really are. The darkness Melinda was in doesn't have to be that way. She could have remembered there is always light and dark. People often have an aversion to the dark, fearing what happens in those spaces. Yet nature is constantly showing us the way. Let me ask you this, when you are sitting on the beach at sunrise, are you worrying about the darkness on the other side of the world?

The permission I gave myself to be different meant I could speak my mind, being labelled 'quirky' and 'different' didn't stop me being vocal when needed. In human design I am a projector, a 4/6, intuitive, a natural teacher and can be bitter when I don't feel heard or appreciated.

I am an empath, intuitive and teacher by nature. I love researching information down to the last detail, mostly so I can be right when feeling misunderstood or judged by so-called intellectuals. I've always listened to the call of my heart, struggling with those more linear in their thoughts and processes. The universe guides me and when it doesn't feel good, I know it's because I am trying to live to the beat of another's drum. I follow the breadcrumbs, trusting.

For many years, I got lost, forgot myself, pretending to be someone else, being who I thought others wanted me to be. I was living life as a generator (modelling my mother), a mad woman ignoring my call to be still, to do nothing, to be alone, volunteer, live in abundance, knowing I would be taken care of no matter what.

I fought against the establishment wherever I could, yet somehow I was still dragged into it, kicking and screaming. My mother used to say 'you can't buck the system', I would say, 'try me'.

Many people are in a state of amnesia, with evidence all around. I was too, until I woke up. I'm sure you have also watched people retire and either become sick, depressed or die. I wondered why others could not see this. People largely identify themselves with what they do, rather than who they are. Melinda identified herself unimportant, a toy for her father, a blip on the radar of surrounding chaos.

I have worked as a cook, bank clerk, hotel cleaner, yoga teacher, belly dance teacher, mother, real estate agent, property developer, trauma coach, sound healer, tour guide, author and wife. I am proud of my achievements, yet I am none of these things. It is more useful to say, *I have cooked, I have taught yoga, I have mothered, I have coached,* etc.

We are all human beings, but in our humanness resides a spiritual being. The universe is constantly giving us nudges in the right direction. If we don't hear them, the universe will keep guiding us. I want to show people that.

Who am I? I am a woman with deep intuition and a fierce fire burning to wake women of the world up to the knowing and remembrance of who they are.

I am that, *So hum.*

This is the next story I want written for women ...

Women are the keepers of ancestral knowledge. We carry the information of remedies, cures for all things, even broken hearts. We are creators and menders. We put things right when we follow our purest hearts. We can be great manipulators but are much more powerful when we manifest.

I want women to know themselves fully and completely. To be more in their feminine energy, so they can hear the call of their hearts, the longing to remember and heal the world with their song. I want women to drop the fight against the masculine and join forces – instead of seeing each other as competition, reunite as sisters.

Women need to remember all life sprung forth from them; without women, there would be no men, no life. Imagine a world with a mass infusion of full Shakti power, all women remembering they hold the mystery of life within their womb.

Yes, I want all women to remember who they are.

This is the next story I am writing for myself ...

My story looks like this: to show up with the highest vibration and remembrance so I can allow other women to see and understand what is possible. How do I do this? To know myself, to find my passion and follow it with all my heart. There is no need for me to hide my power, I am safe, I am powerful, I am a woman. This is my mantra. Knowing it is my superpower.

Rina Mittiga

57 | From: Adelaide, Australia | Lives: Adelaide, Australia

Like a Phoenix rising from the ashes, I am coming out of the fire with a new identity. This has only been possible because I gave myself permission to change my mind.

This is who I am in the world ...

I am Rina Mittiga, founder and director of The Global Luxury Institute, an international motivational speaker, holistic business coach and healer and a business owner who has been a leader in the beauty industry for over three decades.

I help female leaders transform, heal and expand their business into their next level using a combination of business, strategy and energy work ... this is who I THOUGHT I was until I started peeling back the layers of who I REALLY am in the world, and I learned that I am so much more.

My awakening began twenty-seven years ago when I became a mother. My life would never be the same. I created human life and was responsible for this life. We are powerful beings. We have the ability to create life, a planet, a universe!

I was taken on a journey of personal growth, emotional healing and spiritual awakening. I was confronted by my demons and was taught patience, unconditional love and the need to let go of control. I forgot who I was. I was a mother, lover, wife, daughter, sister, friend and employee, and I had this deep urge to return to me. I needed to remember that I was not who everyone else wanted me to be, and that was truly scary.

For generations, we as women have been conditioned to be and look a certain way, often living as a second-hand citizen. As children we are told to silence our voices and only speak when spoken to. We are told we are too much.

A deep realisation hit me on the head recently whilst listening to a conversation between two profound change makers. My sister was the pioneer, the rebel, and paved the way for me to be more of myself, too much, my true self today as an adult. Sacred contracts that I could not comprehend were in motion.

This journey of awakening continued slowly as I ignored the signs many times over.

My path continued in the corporate world where I was very successful in the area of education and sales. I won many awards and led businesses to achieve industry recognition, but I was not happy. There was a dull feeling inside me; I always felt there had to be more than this. I climbed the corporate ladder, led teams and developed businesses.

My dark night of the soul occurred in my fiftieth year. I left a job that was literally soul destroying, my husband lost his job, it was Christmas time and I pretended to my two children that all was well.

All my darkness came up to the surface:

Fear.

Anxiety.

Resentment.

Anger.

I was brought to my knees with desperation, and I completely surrendered. This is when my life began to turn around. My path continued forward, and I began to ask the questions. *There must be more than this* … I launched my amazing website and online coaching for women in beauty, but it never felt true to me.

This year has been deeply transformational for me, and my identity as the beauty business leader is dying. This has been a hard process, as I deeply thought this was who I am. This is all I have known. Then this happened …

I was watching a piece on how thirteen-year-old girls are filtering and changing their appearance before they post on social media. This hit me deep in my heart! What are we teaching our girls? As women, it is time to reclaim our sovereignty, our voices, our beauty – from within.

True beauty comes from within; it is our soul essence. It is the love we have for ourselves. True beauty emanates from your heart and shines out for the world to see. It lights up a room when you enter.

Like a phoenix rising from the ashes, I am coming out of the fire with a new identity. This has only been possible because I gave myself permission to change my mind. It is okay that I create another identity, my true identity, who I came to this earth to be in this time. I also give you permission to change your mind as many times as you want.

This is the next story I want written for women ...

I can no longer sit back as women all around the world continue to struggle with emotional support, relationships and financial security. I want to empower women to be able to step up and create the life of success and freedom that they desire and envision for themselves.

I want to share my gifts and talents so, as women, we can stand shoulder to shoulder and rise together and celebrate each other. I want women to realise they don't have to wait for a man to save them or rely on a man for money; they have the ability and power to save themselves.

This is the next story I am writing for myself ...

I am writing my story of sovereignty, frequency and fortune. I am creating a ripple effect in the world so more and more women can be reached. I am creating my empire so that I am able to transform more and more lives. I am stepping out of fear and into courage, visibility and leadership.

I am creating a life that I don't need to take a holiday from, that gives me joy and that drives my passion, my purpose and my reason for being on this planet. I want to be the pioneer for the next generation of women and pass on the baton of hope, strength, prosperity and voice and break the cycle of poverty and silence.

It is time for the divine feminine to rise together and remember who we are and why we were created. It is divine timing that we are here on this planet now.

It is time to speak up, have a voice and shine from within!

You are beautiful,
Rina xxx

Laura Coburn

32 | From: Melbourne, Australia | Lives: Melbourne, Australia

The world is our playground in which we can create anything and everything, and by choosing to align with love, hopefully, we can leave it better for future generations.

This is who I am in the world ...

On a childhood family holiday, I recall browsing a gift shop and being very drawn to a small, shiny figurine of the Buddha.

There was something in his smile and his unashamedly large belly which brought out an inner smile in me. We are, after all, absorbers and reflectors of the vibes and the world around us, if we allow ourselves to be. I picked up the Buddha as my father had previously hinted that he might buy us *one* small souvenir if we wanted. This jolly smiling figurine was the thing that I wanted. I recall my parents deliberating on whether to buy it for me due to the fact that we were a Christian, church-attending family. I lost interest in the physical figurine and became intrigued by the discussion this miniature smiling man had instigated between my parents. An inner curiousness was sparked within me about what Buddha knew that made him so happy and what more there was to this wisdom. Could I have the same joyful vibe as the Buddha figurine? Were there other happy people I could learn from?

This was the beginning of me learning to listen to 'vibes' or 'feelings' or 'language of the heart'.

Later in life, I read and picked up books about Buddhism and also found myself drawn to other modes of spiritual inquiry or philosophical musings about 'everything': humanity, nature, the universe, existence, behaviour, history, ways of being. Specific areas of study that I have explored in more detail include psychology, yoga and permaculture, but I know that I'll keep growing and expanding in different areas that attract me.

I thought that all humans experienced a spiritual and existential curiosity, but now I suspect that humans stumble across the teachings they need at different times of their life and in slightly different ways. Often this comes when one is healing from something. Part of the healing process of any infliction of the heart, mind or body involves a softening, a relaxation, an acceptance, compassion and then finally an openness. An openness to the new and the ability to embrace and enjoy it.

I have learnt more and more, through my inquisitive openness, to trust and listen to myself and to also connect with the abundant wisdom of nature and the natural world.

I always loved looking after younger children, and from when I was able to, I experienced an embodied desire to give birth. A baby started growing inside me unexpectedly when I was in the middle of a fairly disorganised relationship and an immature stage of my life. I didn't feel ready to be a mother or to give this baby the life that it deserved, so after much deliberation and some consolation from my partner (in another country at the time) I decided to privately book an abortion. Due to the baby's age, it unfortunately needed to be a surgical procedure. As time ticked on closer to the procedure date, or maybe following the date, I can't be sure … I had a vivid dream of my future baby and their sweet face, big brown eyes and softly curled hair.

Of course, this made it harder to recover from the experience of letting go.

During later moments of self-doubt, I doubted whether I would ever be a mother again.

As an initial part of my healing journey, and a solace for myself, I grew a deep reverence for sunsets and cherished this moment of the day and the colours and messages that the sky would treat me with. I didn't know it, but I was learning to listen to the natural world.

Another part of my healing journey has involved me spending more time in nature and in the garden, learning about plants.

When I became intimate with nature, literally, through gardening – touching and caring for soil and plants and the network of life that sustains me, others, and in fact, the whole world – I could more clearly understand the role of the 'mother' that all women have available to them and the beauty of the act of service of mothering. I began to understand the many ways of being a mother. Mothering yourself, mothering the earth, mothering soil, plants, insects, bees, birds, cats, cows, mothering family members and friends, even mothering strangers, in a particular way. Mothering a child I'd given birth to wasn't the only way for me to embody this role.

This is the next story I want written for women ...

Society may try to distract you, pull at your attention/time/money/resources/health/energy … but *try* to keep coming back to *you*, listening to yourself, the calling of your heart and the hearts of the world.

Heart is, after all, a re-jumbled misspelling of the word earth.

Listen to your heart and listen to the earth.

Remember the integrity of your role in the world, of being a caretaker of hearts, carrier of seeds, cultivator of nourishment and enabler of love – in and from yourself and others.

This is the next story I am writing for myself ...

Part of a vision that I experienced in the early days of the pandemic was of our lives in a future world involving deeper connection, respect and reverence for the natural world, and a sense of community which was so content that there was a healthy creative buzz stirring and interactions were from a heart-centred place of love.

As the Dalai Lama says, our societies need to remember that we are all one big family, 'We're all brothers and sisters: physically, mentally and emotionally the same … after all, every one of us is born the same way and dies the same way.'

As for my place in this future vision, I can remember not to fear love or suffering, because the more that we can gracefully and effortlessly allow our hearts to love and to break open, the more light and love can shine through the cracks, the more twinkles we can hold in our eyes and the more golden light we can surround ourselves with as we embody love and bravely walk into the unknown.

Love.

Asia Raine

56 | From: Utah, USA | Lives: Utah, USA

If I can inspire others to trust in their sense of wonder and magic and invite them along as travel companions, I believe we can step beyond ourselves into the grandeur of dreams yet to be lived.

This is who I am in the world …

I feel like I shimmy in and out of labels as I evolve, and I've noticed there are a few that have found a home with me. I am a visionary, mentor, mother, business owner, silversmith, artisan, mediator, survivor, podcast host, teacher and lover. I am a truth bringer. I've been known as a catalyst, been called a troublemaker and have befriended discernment. I've learned that peace exists in balance between dark and light.

I am a survivor of occult ritualistic abuse, human trafficking, medical experimentation and mind control. As I've healed my traumas, I live as one who has reclaimed herself, chooses sovereignty over servitude and practices alignment with God. I learned to recalibrate the darkest frequencies, attune to a greater version of myself and do my best to commune with deity while respecting the diversity of humanness.

Recovering my truth took time. Often, I felt like I was hacking my way through a jungle with a pocketknife. I had forgotten entire experiences, leaving nightmares, random physical conditions and behaviour patterns the only clues to the truth. These shadows developed into depression which actually was the gateway to my healing.

Being born into a blood-cult system allowed my handlers access to me for thirty-seven years. The process of sifting through the traumatic memories was much like being an inner archaeologist, sometimes diving deep, excavating huge chunks of memories and other times gingerly sifting through tiny details. Eight years of hypnotherapy enabled me to extract myself from the relationships, patterns and programs designed to keep me mentally imprisoned, and I witnessed myself stretch into the space of authenticity where I can flourish. This kind of personal cleansing has empowered my voice and increased my capacity to empathetically hold space for others in powerful ways.

At first I didn't recognise I was paving a way for others to do the same, but as I look back I can see my journey has done just that. Many can relate to being exploited, lied to, seduced and misled, and yet I feel we are the jubilant, mystical ones who can create life beyond those limitations. I celebrate as others courageously champion themselves and inspire courage in those around them.

This is the next story I want written for women ...

I consider the art of observation a superpower. It's not the easiest thing to be the witness, the one who watches as others struggle or hurt. This perspective has required me to hold love as the umbrella over people as they experience the storms that challenge them. It asks me to believe in their capabilities and resilience more than the doubt threatening to wash away their faith.

Women are natural nurturers, and the impulse to intervene is strong. We can jump in with good intentions to teach and guide, to buffer or save. But we can also criticise, control, coerce and punish. These reactions are often well-developed and heavily anchored within societal and familial tethers, and it takes desire and focus to unhook from such habits.

I want women to witness life with grace and courage. Knowing there is no need to turn away from the unbearable and instead alchemise it, drawing value from any circumstance to transform it. Injustice can be the fuel to create change.

We are acquainted with the victim, villain and hero triangle from our earliest experiences and may not recognise how often we identify as one of them.

It takes courage to exit those stories and choose a different perspective, practicing patience with ourselves through the process. Learning to recognise what our hearts adore and move with total trust towards it, joyfully pursuing our dreams and embracing the unpredictable organic nature of living as a participant, not as one who suffers from it.

There are no rules that promise life will be painless or free of unfairness or discrimination, but beauty can still be the overgarment if we choose to dance with nature, our undomesticated mother.

This is the next story I am writing for myself ...

I was inspired to explore the craft of metalsmithing after a trip to Ireland where I was a part of a woman's cooperative helping local women make items from island resources. Silversmithing intrigued me and taught me the language of alchemy. The elements of fire, air, water and earth came together to show me that the path to mastery is actually a series of mistakes accumulating into wisdom.

I write my story day by day, and it's clear a new chapter has begun sprouting from a desire to establish a location where self-led healing is the norm. Where teachers and practitioners are just as dedicated to their own healing journey as those who are just beginning theirs. Where support for the self-motivated seeker of personal truth is honoured and celebrated and the seeds of creativity can enrich the process.

I desire to leave a legacy that stimulates society to mature spiritually in unique and diverse ways authentic to each soul. Where the rightful place of instinctual growth is valued and nurtured. I recognise my place in this world as one of its most determined guardians, assertively engaging with life, knowing we are strongest as we call forward recruits when in need and stand fiercely alone if required, to hold sacred space for self and others. I've come to realise that chaos and questions are the playground of initiation and have moved from the territory of self-doubt and mistrust to the wild wilderness of creation – a land that is ever changing and often requires radical surrender to the unseen as my guide.

My story is one of curiosity, creativity and courage as I continue to follow my inner compass. If I can inspire others to trust in their sense of wonder and magic and invite them along as travel companions, I believe we can step beyond ourselves into the grandeur of dreams yet to be lived.

Jenny Chiu

37 | From: Hong Kong | Lives: Melbourne, Australia

I want to be associated with hope, power and love, as I build bridges between cultures.

This is who I am in the world ...

When I came to Australia twenty years ago, my language was a factor that made me 'not good enough', creating many misunderstandings and negative feelings because of the cultural barriers between Hong Kong and Australia. I became frustrated at myself because I had limited vocabulary and expression in English, and I did not always explain things in the most appropriate ways. I would realise afterwards what I should have said yet could not convey. Raised in Hong Kong, I was bullied for my appearance, as I was considered 'big' for an Asian woman, and Australia provided a different set of challenges in finding belonging.

I thank God for giving me this new beginning. I believed, *the old has gone, the new is here* – this new life experience in a new country gave me hope and a new identity as Jenny Chiu.

It has become my passion to be the bridge between Australian and Chinese culture and language, because we all want to be understood. As my English improved, I had a stirring feeling of how good it would be to be a person who could harmonise these barriers between people.

When I began working in corporate, I realised that a very high level of language was required, and I was teased for my grammar, being told that 'no-one talks like you' – because classroom English is no longer 'good enough'. I was mistaken for other Asian girls, and I felt sorrow when they did not remember my name. I became scared of going to work and that I had to work doubly hard to prove myself. At that stage in my identity development, I was not proud of being from Hong Kong, and being a trilingual person gave me no benefits in my career advancement.

I took a year off to travel to Europe and my perception of myself changed drastically. As a traveller, my accent was not shameful and I came to see it as beautiful, as everyone was saying the same things in different accents. I found that an accent gives clues about a person, like an atlas of one's background and travels. When I returned from Europe, everyone was more interested in where I had been and how I had adopted 'the accent', rather than in looking at my differences in a negative way.

On my return, a friend asked me to host his wedding as a multilingual master of ceremony (MC) – a paid gig. I had been praying for a clean slate and questioning whether there was a bigger world beyond the nine-to-five corporate life. I wondered if people would pay me as a host who can translate. I set up a simple Facebook page as I accepted the gig. I had been in Australia for ten years and was ready to create the next part of my life here. I had become fluent in understanding the nuances between English, Mandarin and Cantonese, and my year-long travel experience gave me confidence in dealing with difficult situations for positive outcomes. I felt that I had a lot to offer in harmonising the dynamics and relationships for people interacting between different languages.

In 2019, I had built up my multilingual wedding MC business and it felt like the best time to sustain myself without working in corporate, but then COVID-19 happened. Everything that was running stopped or derailed. I needed a breakthrough. During the lockdowns I channelled my energy into fitness and health, something that I had never been successful with throughout the years. My body felt like the only thing left in my control. *I am going to do something more ridiculous than COVID-19 is doing to me.* I wanted a transformed self, and I lost 14kg and two clothing sizes in eleven months. I am truly thankful that this crisis turned into a blessing that healed my early scars from when I had been bullied because of my appearance.

Today I am very happy to host weddings, serve people, help to share their stories of love and bridge the gap of language, culture and even generations. Previously I was scared of relationships and love and for many years, I did not believe that these were possible and a lot has shifted through being an MC and witnessing love. It is my greatest wish to each couple that I can provide blessings for their lives together.

There are a lot of misunderstandings when interacting between Asians, and I want to help the Australian community build trust with the Asian community by easing this communication and improving their understanding of one another.

This is the next story I want written for women ...

I hope that as women we can all take something that has been a difficult experience and both know that it will not last forever, and that it can become something powerful to give to others. I never would have imagined that I would be an MC at Chinese and English weddings through something as trivial as opening a Facebook page, putting up one post and taking up the offer to host one friend's wedding. If I did not start from zero, nothing would have happened, just like my weight loss project as well.

I wanted a change, so I did something different, and change happened. I have so much passion and joy, and I am paid well for it. I have found the sweet spot. It is my wish that more women take the first steps and keep going, because so much is possible.

This is the next story I am writing for myself ...

I am now glad that 'no-one talks like me' because this has become my blessing for many people. I want to continue to be a testament of bringing people hope and miracles. I want to be Jenny Chiu, someone who is remembered in the Asian-Australian community for doing an amazing job with weddings, funerals and other events. I want to be associated with hope, power and love as I build bridges between the cultures.

And I want to write my own love story, with God holding my pen.

Bianca Caruana

36 | From: Sydney, Australia | Lives: Between Malta and alongside my backpack

I want women to find that special place of stillness where the dialogue is simply between them and their higher selves.

This is who I am in the world ...

I am a thirty-six years young Australian-Maltese woman born and raised in Sydney, Australia, but for the most part of the last seven years, have been galivanting around the globe with a backpack, a free spirit and an open heart. I tend to feel the world more than I see it, navigating my way through this incarnation with an intuitive compass and a deep level of trust that there is magic behind each fleeting moment.

I am a creative soul. Words are the colours I paint with. My canvas is poetry, reflective writing, journalism and blogging. You may find me under the alias of The Altruistic Traveller, a project that existed to explore the intersection of travel and sustainability but ultimately facilitated the exploration of my own internal constitution. It became apparent what I was seeking outwardly was a reflection of what I was seeking inwardly which was ultimately unconditional love and compassion.

It wasn't until later in life that I started to tap into my creative energies. They were suppressed because, for a long time, I existed according to society's expectations of me, expectations fabricated by a thousand years of patriarchy. The benchmarks I felt measured against were the status of my career, the status of my relationships and the status of my bank account. But in my mid-thirties, I let go of those expectations and started to live according to what made me feel aligned.

I think of my soul like a river, and where that river flows freely is where I follow.

If there is ever an obstruction in my flow, I recognise it as a lesson or opportunity to observe and re-evaluate which direction to take.

This is the next story I want written for women ...

Just as I was able to navigate my own personal trenches to meet the woman I am today, I, too, wish for women to find that innate treasure and become who they want to be in this world – to be who they are and not who others expect them to be. Oftentimes there are so many expectations holding us down and keeping us small. We are told we need to dress this way, or have this career, or have three children, or marry by the time we are twenty-five, or know what we want to be when we grow up, or have short hair, or have long hair, or paint our nails, or don't paint our nails. But who made these rules? Why is everyone wanting to weigh in on what we look like, what we do and who we are?

The story I next want to be written for women is the freedom to write our own unique stories. I want women to find that special place of stillness where the dialogue is simply between them and their higher selves. I want a celebration of individuality, for women to look at one another and say, 'You do you, girl! I'll be here cheering you on!' I want us women to set our own benchmarks and to be no longer governed by the benchmarks of a patriarchal society or of others. When we decide what is best for us, when we set the goalposts, we *will* score. But to know ourselves we must go within, and ask, *Who am I in this world without what others expect of me?*

I would like to share a poem I wrote called *Within* about my journey back to self. May we all have the courage to be who we truly want to be in this world.

>Nice to meet you, I said
>I admire your strength
>You have courage and patience
>I once only dreamt
>You stand tall and move forward with passion, yet grace
>Your rivers are flowing, there is light on your face
>And it emanates to all of the people around

And to me, I can see, there is something you've found
It's something I was searching, a long while ago
A gem in the sand, a stone in the snow
I looked under, and over, past mountains, 'round bends
And wandered, miles yonder, to the rainbow's end
The journey was thorough
but also quite long
I got tired and weathered
Lost the words to my song
May I ask you to help me
To teach me what you know
To move forward with strength
With the peace that you show
Well, you see, darling girl, you can pass rainbow's end
And another, and another, it's an infinite ascend
Or you can feel with your heart, put your toes in the sand
And know all you need is right where you stand
Life is here, it is now
You have more than you know
Look inside, not out there
Close your eyes and let go
Listen in to the sound of the voices within
The way trees talk to roots, and clouds talk to wind
There you'll find all the answers you've been searching for
And the light that is dim will shine once more
Oh, thank you! I said, full of joy and much glee
Then I noticed
There was something familiar to me
I saw who she was
This woman was me

This is the next story I am writing for myself ...

Today, I am a woman who endeavours to show up in the world as simply herself, removed from any veils or facades. Each day I hold gratitude for what is, I find trust that all is as it is intended to be, and let my intuition guide me to where it is my river is flowing.

As I shed the layers of myself that no longer serve me and live each day as my true authentic self, I wake up each morning in peace and presence knowing I have given my all to this life.

We leave a million tiny legacies, but in the end, we all become stories, so they may as well be written in our own words.

Anne Carr

48 | From: Western Australia | Lives: Melbourne, Australia

Helen Keller once quoted, 'The only thing worse than being blind, is having sight but no vision.' We have to believe in our goals and hold on to our vision without letting this be obscured by anyone else.

This is who I am in the world ...

I am a spiritual goddess, a mother and a mentor/influencer for my son Harry, a wife, friend, sister, healer and lover of crystals, words of wisdom and quotes. I'm a seeker of knowledge, a big kid at heart and passionate about people and life. I'm a lover of plants, nature and exquisite cars and a sponsor for children and guide dogs. I'm kind, honest, faithful, sensitive, funny, intelligent, and I wear my heart on my sleeve.

I have a great sense of humour; I love my own company and I take pride in my independence. I left my old self back in Western Australia with four suitcases, a one-way ticket and my little red car on the back of a truck to start life anew in Melbourne. When younger, I was influenced by others; however, growing up means that I have followed my own path and am no longer easily influenced by others.

My life, like many, has been influenced by childhood trauma, by no fault of my own or my late parents. I fell under the spell of a rock-spider-grown-adult that shaped the early years of my life and into my later years. I knew about sexuality from a very young age, understanding things little girls shouldn't know until they are much older. I missed out on some of my childhood emotional and psychological needs being met, and it shows in my maturity and the ways I behave at times.

I have felt the impact of this throughout my life and it has heavily affected my self-esteem and confidence. When at school, I was bullied and wanted to crawl into the curb of shame – shame of being me and self-pity of who I was – which resulted in me leaving school after year nine, barely able to read or write. My spirit was crushed; I was broken. I didn't want to be on earth, feeling that this place was cruel and I wanted out, as only the smart people could make it in this thing we call LIFE. Those I saw as A-graders, the rich kids, the university graduates, not me, I was never going to amount to much – that's what I believed.

I was insecure and I lacked self-worth. I didn't have a voice and I was too scared to speak for fear of being laughed at, criticised and ridiculed.

In the late 1980s and early 1990s when I was in my late teens, I picked up a copy of Louise Hay's *You Can Heal Your Life* and *The Power is Within You*. I taught myself to read, write and understand words as I listened to the tape recordings and read the words in the books. I continued reading personal and spiritual development books. This self-discovery taught me what I needed to build my self-worth, and from here, many doors and opportunities have opened for me. Life has since happened *for* me, not *to* me.

It has taken until my late forties to see myself as strong, independent, successful and savvy. Personal development has become an obsession. I have learnt the word PARADIGM, and I am working on changing mine! This has become a daily ritual for me. Once I had the confidence to move to Melbourne at twenty-eight, I did. Since then, I have married, bought property, travelled, built a successful career in real estate, had my son and meditate daily.

This is the next story I want written for women …

I have learned many things on my journey and here are some of the messages that I feel others can also learn from:

Firstly, you are not broken, you're a spiritual being having a physical experience.

Secondly, there is nothing that you CAN'T do, you CAN only try, and if at first you don't succeed, keep going, you've got this. You can do anything that you decide to do.

Thirdly, the great author Helen Keller once quoted, 'The only thing worse than being blind is having sight but no vision.' I went through life thinking that I didn't have any goals or desire, yet we all have sight. We have to believe in our goals and hold on to our vision without letting this be obscured by anyone else. I wish I had been taught this at an early age.

Fourth, you have a voice, and even if it shakes, speak to those you trust so that you are heard and have the chance to be believed.

Fifth, honour your body and yourself because you are beautiful exactly as you are. You don't need the surgery or body transformation that we are brainwashed about through our lives in weekly magazines – be slim, be tanned, get yourself a melanoma just in time for Christmas. We all have a responsibility to embed in the younger generation of today that perfection and fitting in should not set the standard of what it is to be a woman.

Sixth, we all have a gift; even if you haven't found it yet, it is there and it will come to light. Sometimes trauma means that it takes a while to uncover these gifts.

Seventh, I never returned to school and or got that university degree, yet I went on to have a successful career in the retail industry and then in real estate, managing over $136 million in property and upward counting. Where you begin is not necessarily where you end.

Eighth, while there will be challenges, keep going. There is a reason for your experiences and lessons that will contribute to helping other people, and it's the ability to help change another's life that makes our own transformation worth it.

This is the next story I am writing for myself ...

My next story is to teach what has helped me to reinstate my self-worth and leave a legacy to others. I want to sponsor guide dogs and support children's charities. Finally, I want to raise my son so that rather than getting over his childhood, he is free to be a confident dreamer and live his wildest life! My greatest lesson in this is that his freedom starts with me. What I want for myself, I want for you, too.

Stephanie Siefkas

42 | Born: Colorado, USA | Lives: Missouri, USA

Alchemist. Adventurer. Naturalist. It's my invitation for every woman to choose and create freely.

'Trying to define yourself is like trying to bite your own teeth.' Alan Watts

This is who I am in the world ...

As a child, I was trained by the world to let it tell me who I am. A smart mouth, a troublemaker and a daydreamer. While it's true that our reality is a reflection of us, this statement oversimplifies one of the deepest truths of the human condition. We are more than what the world believes us to be. We are the collection of stories we tell, the stories others tell about us … and we are none of that at all. We are more than our unrealised gifts and untapped potential, amongst a mosaic of life's experiences … and we are all divinely designed and unique.

We are infinite, limitless beings, who have misunderstood who we are for a very long time and are finally remembering.

For most of my life, I've been the definition of misunderstood. I've been called a manipulator, a risk-taker and an extremist … and my ever-healing inner child loves the way those words are now translated by my inner voice.

I was the young girl who saw good in everyone despite skin colour or socioeconomic status. I was the rebellious teen who brought my love for others to life, often in 'forbidden' relationships that challenged society's standard for a 'little white girl in Small Town USA'. I was the single mother who reached for every solution to heal my daughter, Caliana, from the wrath of pharmaceuticals, screaming from the rooftops to burn down the status quo of health care and informed consent. I was the daughter of neurological disease, manifested in the embodiment of my mother. Her intuitive gifts lived in full remission, barely visible in the shell she became at the hand of Parkinson's.

The deep cell care that I provided her offered visible improvements that did little more than skim the wave of cognitive dissonance present in those people around us. It went unreceived. After she left us, the therapies I sought out for her would be integral in retiring Cali's lung disorder and my twenty-plus year relationship with chronic respiratory illness. The lungs hold grief, and we were clearing it. Our contract was three generations deep, calling forward a new program. A remembering. As my mother left this realm, she opened the gateway to a world of microcosm-macrocosm exploration and the cell to soul connection. Cell food cleansing, DNA activation, Akashic healing and the birth of something entirely new … yet remembered.

The global mission borne in me was conceived through my newly realised gifts and the retirement of old programming that impacts the way we care for our bodies and our earth. It was borne of the journey to healing for both myself and my daughter. It came in the whispers of her grandmother, alongside a beautiful journey through the dark crevices of spiritual awakening. It was Cali who mused my spiritual awakening alongside her own, and it was her grandmother who facilitated the time line exchange and lit the fuse of a spiritual rocket. All of this is rooted in the energy of love and oneness, as distilled through the voices of Mary Magdalene, Mother Mary and Grandmother Anna. My work and mission became clear – cellular health and celestial connection, cell to soul.

When it was time to name my mission and bring my medicine forward … I searched. It would come, as I knew it would, through searches and synonyms. Deeper meaning. I was scouring ancient languages for words like vitality, health and wellness. Hebrew. Greek. Aramaic. And then there it was, as I landed on Sanskrit. My search for wellbeing produced a long list, atop which sat the name of my daughter. The word Kalyana. I didn't make her name up after all … it was embedded and symbolic, to surface at just the perfect moment. And in that, my story came full circle. Synchronicity was speaking to me in ways I'd never heard before. And so, Kalyana Therapeutics was born, and within it a container for cell to soul connection – an expansive online community called The Akashic Kitchen.

This is the next story I want written for women ...

Alchemist. Adventurer. Naturalist. It's my invitation for every woman to choose and create freely.

These are the words that have emerged for me from labels like 'manipulator', 'risk-taker' and 'extremist'. After years of measuring myself against others' judgements, I stripped it down. What was I embodying that wasn't mine and how was it preventing me from accessing my authentic expression? It turns out I was carrying generations of stuck energy, stifled expression and physical toxicity that were keeping me small.

Cellular toxicity buffers our unique energy signature ... and we can choose differently. It's in conscious awareness of our divine design that we reclaim our personal power and stand in our sovereignty.

This is the next story I am writing for myself ...

We create as we speak, and I speak other-worldly abundance into the future, for both myself and the collective. Through the Akashic-based therapies I now live and teach, the opportunity for soul healing and new earth cultivation have drawn me to lay roots with my husband and family in a place called Eden.

In the hills of the Midwest, we're cultivating a healing sanctuary and actively dreaming it into being – a soft landing space and mystery school for deep soul work, woven with energetic and emotional mastery. It's a place for students and teachers to serve, be seen and to see others in their gifts. It's a place for the those who would otherwise have been burned at the stake to reclaim their naturalistic ways and fly in the face of the matrix.

Eden is an activator and amplifier, calling on the energy of rebirth and restoration. It's a reunion with Mother Goddess, and Her timeless earth medicine. It's a call to rediscover oneself, an offering to all ... to reconnect cosmically through self, earth and God.

Kylie Butler

46 | From: Newport Beach, Australia | Lives: Bali, Indonesia

I choose to be eternally curious, in wonder, grateful and believing that the beauty of life is found in conscious connection.

This is who I am in the world ...

I am building a life I don't want to escape from – a life in recovery from alcoholism. Alcoholism and addiction were my 'gifts in shitty wrapping paper', the catalysts for a life of passion, purpose and heart-centred values. I am not defined by my story, but I am proud of the path I've taken and how the darkest times have brought joy, meaning and connection. My deepest wound has transmuted the pain I suffered into helping others.

I'll admit, I am extremely privileged: white, well-educated, Catholic, an attractive and pretty blonde with an Australian passport. My family are extremely loving, supportive and never left me, even in the darkest times. In the cartoon *The Simpsons,* you see two families, the Simpsons (the dysfunctional family) and the Flanders (the perfect family). The Flanders are my family, my dad even has a moustache. I am extremely humbled and grateful for how awesome my family are (not for the moustache!) and for these blessings.

A high-functioning alcoholic with an impressive corporate career as head of people and culture and a HR leader, with a couple of podcasts, many people didn't know I was blackout drinking for days with empty bottles of vodka and wine filling my cupboards and handbag. I ended up in multiple rehabs, destroying my life and having two cancelled weddings, before getting clean, moving to Bali and building a beautiful purpose-led life as an entrepreneur, coach and consultant.

Addiction is a complex neurological condition. Complex trauma + high sensitivity = addiction, most often. We all have 'craving minds': grasping, scanning for threats, wired for survival. In this hyperconnected, disconnected era, where we desperately seek belonging, we numb, dumb and distract with Netflix and chocolate. For the highly sensitive ones with complex childhood trauma, saturated fat and sugar simply aren't enough to fill the empty hole inside, so we go for a needle or bottle of spirits. That was me, straight vodka, physiologically and psychologically addicted.

I otherwise thought I was healthy, driven and happy, and couldn't understand why I couldn't stop. This gift drove my self-discovery and studies, leading to my expertise in addiction, and finally, recovery. I'd always been passionate about helping others and fascinated by the human mind. And then, bingo! My struggles, corporate career, interests, passions and area of genius aligned. My pain and the suffering of my loved ones has not been in vain as I right the wrongs that my misunderstood illness took. I now help others to not fall as deep and come back with profound insights when they do.

My life, family, friends, circumstances, situations – my story – has led to a life filled with juiciness and joy. I've sat on my potential deathbed and looked forward. I know why I'm here and that I want to live my life from love, not fear, from intention and not reaction. I choose to be eternally curious, in wonder, grateful and believing that the beauty of life is found in conscious connection. Conscious connection to oneself, our why, our values, the present moment, to joy surrounding us and deep, profound and beautiful heart-to-hearts with each other. I'm on this planet to inspire, empower and alleviate suffering. I'm here to impact everyone around me positively in the smallest and largest ways.

My home is on the Island of the Gods – Bali – a deeply spiritual island with a balanced lifestyle, surrounded by like-minded souls. I travel and spend time in Oz with my nieces. I am a hopeless romantic with a rich history of beautiful and growth-inducing relationships, and I'm involved in altruistic activities: fundraising and charity work.

This is the next story I want written for women …

I want women to find their creative gifts and passions early and to nurture these, understanding that there are times where we're winning and times when we're learning. Suffering is optional. Pain is not. Thanks, Buddha, for these wise words. Nurturing our mind, body and spirit is right up there with basic hygiene, like brushing our teeth.

We need to celebrate and reach out to others more. Many entrepreneurial women held a hand out to me, and I try to do the same. With an abundance mindset, scarcity barely needs to exist. While said from a privileged position, heaven and hell are in the mind, in our relationship to the external and also ourselves.

I'd love a world where men and women stop trying to be the same and instead celebrate differences as equals. Women are gifted with natural emotional intelligence. This can be a nurtured secret to success, happiness, deeper relationships and a meaningful life.

I have come to appreciate the importance of connection, gratitude and intentional living and would love to see women empowered to not follow societal rules or outdated values that don't serve them.

In cultivating our minds, curating our social circles, intentionally nurturing our gifts and by taking estimable actions aligned to our values, we build self-love, meaning, purpose and joy in our lives. I believe in a better world for humankind through living intentionally.

This is the next story I am writing for myself ...

I seek to ebb and flow like the sea, to not get caught up in the undercurrent and to know peace and bliss. I'm not afraid of dark nights of the soul, and welcome what life throws at me. I simply wish to enjoy, learn, grow and help others on this crazy, crazy journey. I'm excited about stepping into my authentic self and discarding old inhibitions. I desire further self-discovery and a soul partnership.

I look forward to deeper self-love, love for others and the planet. I look forward to making a greater impact, starting with this book.

I'm excited about internal and external growth – feeling free, embodying all aspects of myself, success and abundance. I'm excited about helping others on their path, building my businesses to serve many and further travelling the globe, podcasting and speaking more. I am looking forward to helping many people through From Here On with recovery coaching, exclusive private rehabs and virtual rehabs, and through With A Meaningful Life by Design business and career coaching, I empower and inspire with my podcast.

Penelope Joy

54 | From: Broken Hill, Australia | Lives: Melbourne, Australia

I want the next generations of girls to KNOW WHO THEY ARE, to be bold to speak their truth, to believe in their purpose, to be passionate in discovering it.

This is who I am in the world ...

My personal story seems ordinary, mundane; I am a typical middle-class Aussie girl. I love playing the piano, composing, reading, writing, dancing salsa, hanging out with friends, the ocean, hiking, riding and keeping fit.

As I delve deeper into who I am, I see three significant women.

My mum is a fierce, independent, vibrant and vital woman with incredible energy. I always remember her saying to me, 'You can do anything you want in life; you don't need a man to do it.' What an amazing statement for a woman born in 1938! It was liberating to hear this. Two other things she said that stood out were, 'The Shean women are like black widow spiders, they eat their mate …' and, 'You are Penelope Joy because you are our joy.'

The first is funny, and it gave me permission to be strong; the second was spoken to a young girl, feeling unsure of her place in her family and the world, bringing life and purpose in that moment. I have never forgotten those words spoken to bring life. My mum embodies spirit and strength!

The second woman is my eldest sister, Beth. She is six years older than me. Her quiet, understated determination reveals a different kind of strength to that of my mum. She is kind and loving, generous and good. With her integrity and humble spirit (considering her many accomplishments), she became a role model for me early in life. I looked up to her and aspired to be like her.

The third was my piano teacher, Mrs Van Wezel. Her passion and complete commitment to her craft inspired my love of music, and I flourished as her student.

My mum was a strong positive influence, yet I also watched as her marriage of thirty years crumbled through a long-term affair by my father, and I watched her as a woman crumble. Later, when my own marriage of twenty-five years with four children fell apart, I was determined not to fall apart myself. It has been one of the most challenging and difficult times in my life. Yet, it enabled me to rediscover and reclaim who I am as a woman, who Penelope Joy truly is at her core.

My love of human behaviour and studies in psychology came together during this time and I shifted my vocational focus from music teaching to welfare counselling and coaching. Over the past eight years I have had the privilege of supporting young people and families through their own challenges.

I aspire to be someone who impacts others for good in the world. I KNOW that my piece of this puzzle fits right there in speaking words of life to girls, imparting truth, self-belief and trust in their identity and purpose. I want the next generations of girls to know who they are, to be bold to speak their truth, to believe in their purpose and to be passionate in discovering it.

To feel free to explore and experiment; to not know all the answers straight away; to make mistakes and learn from them; to gather experiences and move inexorably towards fulfilling what they are on this planet to do; always seeing the blessings and being grateful for the wins, trials, challenges and failures because these are the things that shape and build character; to remember constantly who they are, staying connected to source, God, spirit; to discern truth from lies and false beliefs that would erode their identity. THIS!

This is the next story I want written for women ...

My biggest passion is to empower women and girls to have awareness of themselves, a deep understanding of their core values and desires in life, to follow their dreams, live large and be true to their authentic self. To this end, two words immediately jump out: identity and purpose.

In my search for meaning, thousands of moments of contemplation and seeking God, it is in faith, trust, hope and deep, abiding, unconditional love where I have found my identity, who I am, my value and purpose – why I am here at this time on this planet. It is an ever-evolving story.

I believe all that is good and loving, wild, miraculous and wondrous stems from God. Having this bone-deep conviction in my heart defines my purpose as I look at young girls growing up in a complex world, navigating judgements, restrictions, persecution, misrepresentation, shame, a skewed and confused sense of identity, self-worth and value, feeling lost and adrift in the world, battered, damaged, hurt. These girls grow into women who need emotional healing.

I desire to help them understand and regulate their emotions, know they are loved, precious, created for an amazing purpose, that what was said to them and over them by unthinking people is not who they are. I want them to know that they are enough, they belong, they are worthwhile, they have a future with hope. I want to impact them so that they can experience transformation and live fulfilled, happy and joyful lives, bringing up another generation with life, light and love.

This story must also include boys growing into the next generation of men who view, treat and experience girls and women with love, being integral to the story and also healed.

This is the next story I am writing for myself …

I am a transformational coach and mentor. I help women reclaim their identity, their essence and beauty, the parts of themselves that have been lost through their core relationships with themselves, their partners, children, work colleagues, friends and family. My joy and passion are for them to find healing and wholeness in their relationships through the development of strong emotional intelligence and being empowered through discovering their soul purpose for service on earth.

Through my journey, I have birthed a twelve-week course called 'Reclaim You' for women who, like myself, have lost key parts of themselves to relationships, family, children. It is a deep call to healing and wholeness and to reclaim their power, passion and purpose in life as they develop strong emotional intelligence – to come back to their authentic self.

I want to see God lift the lid on this thing – to see a global movement of reclamation. To see governments fund programs, courses, seminars, retreats and camps on a large scale; to see women and girls in developing nations empowered to be all they are called to be.

This is my soul purpose and I love it!

Much love and blessings,

Penny xx

Mandy Terbrueggen

31 | From: Florida, USA | Lives: Florida, USA

I'm a soul with a divide, longing for two worlds, both in a community and to be free from roots.

This is who I am in the world ...

I'm a soul with a divide, longing for two worlds, both in a community and free from roots. We are designed to be in tribes, partnerships; we flourish when we give and receive support. After too long, my heart desires to spread wider and see more, any other way would be dull and untrue. Going far outside my comfort zone and embracing a new culture is the most profound way to grow.

After three years of living in New York City, hustle and noise, and being in an environment that is focused on money, I walked away, packed a couple of bags and headed for a destination the opposite of Manhattan: Bali, Indonesia. Here, I first felt the heightened awareness travelling solo brings, needing to dig deep and think differently.

I arrived to a wave of humidity and incense. Acclimatising to the jungle, I met someone who suggested I check out dating apps to meet people. I met a guy, also from the United States, and we took a yoga class at Yoga Barn, grabbing dinner with his friends after. Thrilled I had met new people, I instantly felt confident about using 'the apps'. It was easy and platonic ... walking down the street, his friends ahead of us. Coming to a narrow, broken part of the sidewalk, he stops and lets me pass. As I pass, he gropes my ass. Having not touched previously, I was stunned and acted like it didn't happen. I spent another hour with him and his friends. I don't know why I didn't say anything, but wished I had. I didn't expect this in Bali.

In my fifth country and in month four of solo travel, I was still not used to the alone time, but I had experienced moments of pure bliss where I got lost in beautiful surroundings. I was in Rotorua, New Zealand. I decided to run to Whakarewarewa Forest, three miles away and explore, losing track of time, exploring in the beautiful redwoods. I headed back, very slowly. Arriving at the hostel, the front doors were open, and I didn't see a single traveller. I clambered up the stairs to my room, the door was open, beds stripped and my things – gone. Downstairs, I found an irritated host, informing me they had closed for cleaning, preparing for a school group. I completely forgot about check-out time and panicked. Handed a laundry basket with my unpacked suitcase, half my things spilling out, she said I needed to leave. After five hours of running and hiking, I was exhausted. I sat outside the hostel with my things and repacked my suitcase.

Feeling my day couldn't get worse, a guy walked up to me and said, 'You got a lot of shit, huh.' I looked up, haphazardly responding in exhaustion. I saw how ridiculous it was and realised I could only laugh. We chatted and discovered we were both travelling solo on a similar route, making our way down the North Island to the South. He offered me a ride to the bus station, turning my horrible morning into a new friendship, crossing paths throughout our travels in New Zealand and beyond!

If I went back in time, I would tell my seventeen-year-old self that everything is more enjoyable once you lean into who you are, riding the wave rather than forcing things to happen. I thought that after my sabbatical I would have all the answers about who I was, what I wanted to do and had started doing it. While I didn't find them all, the learning through moments like that did not compare to three and half years in college or three years living in New York City.

This is the next story I want written for women ...

Travel is the soul's way of finding who we are without the distraction of societal norms, an unexplainable passion of mine planted in my heart, never quite leaving.

As females, it seems we live in a constant state of contrast that rings truer through travel. Telling people that I travel solo is met with, 'Wow you're so brave,' or, 'Oh, aren't you scared to travel alone as a female?' I never understood why others thought fear should stop me, when a bigger part of me felt I didn't have a choice but to learn in this way.

Travel shows us how to push aside outdated traditions, open our minds and learn how other cultures make room for women, and where we, especially in the USA, need to bring chairs to the table for the biggest impact. This is my desire for women – that they build a life that allows them to learn and grow through experiencing worlds beyond their own.

This is the next story I am writing for myself ...

I've learned the best way to honour myself is to be flexible to the season of life I am in, slowing down and listening to my heart. What did happen on that sabbatical was beginning a journey of travelling deeper and discovering more. The best way I've found is to give through service, time and energy. Longing to give back to the countries I visited, as they had given to me, I tried to do some service there. I learned that it was not as easy as I thought to connect with organisations and volunteer as I did not hear back until I had already left that region.

In early 2019, I created Travel Gives with the desire to help people give back and get involved locally while journeying to new destinations. This, too, has been a journey in itself, starting as one thing and evolving since. Riding the wave and letting things flow naturally, my journey has now taken me to a place I never dreamed of that feels beyond fulfilling for this season.

I've found community, combined with my marketing and athletics experience, while having the chance to make an impact with student athletes here in the USA. Travel is and always will be one of my biggest passions, but 2020 showed me above all else that what I most value is connection and learning with others, and this season is teaching me how to cultivate that even deeper.

Julie Scollary

54 | From: Australia | Lives: Bendigo, Victoria, Australia

We teach kids academia and not life skills, nor do we have them sit with community elders ... I believe in human rights and us all understanding each other, returning to our basics in sitting, talking and listening.

'The journey of a thousand miles begins with a single step.' Lao Tzu

This is who I am in the world ...

As a small child I would record myself on tape saying that no-one is going to hurt me anymore in the voice of the wicked witch. I also resonated with the character Dorothy from *The Wizard of Oz* and the paths that she walked – as my own has been quite rugged. Like a tornado, my own healing has taken the time it takes for a small, developing, yet crushed mind, soul and spirit to recover.

The land of Oz turned upside down, the Scarecrow, the Tin Man, the yellow brick road and Toto were my safe, secure space to go. I would put on my red shoes and click my heels and imagine my healing journey. If I were to pass from this world tomorrow, the legendary status I would leave behind is that I was my own hero – true to myself and full of gratitude for this life, even with its challenges.

As a survivor of childhood trauma, sexual assault, rape, institutional abuse and multiple medical traumas from my career as a paramedic, I was predisposed to depression, complex post-traumatic stress disorder (CPTSD), anxiety and suicidal ideations in my adult years. Choosing to work in crisis-driven professions helping others, I sunk deeper and deeper. Developing the new me has been the slow unfolding journey of fulfilment and passion that highlights triumph over tragedy.

After twenty-four years as an intensive care paramedic, a catalyst event caused me to reach breaking point. I required intensive psychological therapy as an inpatient in a mental health facility. This was the darkest, loneliest and most isolating time in my life. I never imagined that this would happen to me, in a career that I had dedicated my heart and soul to, yet I knew so little about caring for myself.

Loneliness and being alone are two very different things. In that psychiatric ward in 2005, I was in the shower with the water running over me, like I was sitting at the bottom of a well. At this moment I felt thunderstruck, and I was lucky to have people retrieve me. I made a choice not to set myself up to continually be traumatised anymore.

At the age of fifty I said no more nursing, disability support work and paramedicine. It was time to focus on me and create a new adventure. I was waking from my slumber, much like sleeping beauty, determined and prepared to heal. I became a mental health advocate with Code 9 Foundation, offering me growth as I shared my experiences and learnings with other emergency services workers also showing signs of PTSD, depression and anxiety. Imparting what I have learned about resilience and self-care, I remind them that their uniform doesn't make them a superhero.

My healing involved psychotherapy, being around like-minded positive people, mindfulness eye movement dissociation reprocessing (EMDR), focus on the now, some medication, self-care and nurturance, acknowledging where I'm at and challenging myself. Mindset work has been huge in becoming a more authentic version of myself in the world.

I now do charity work with assistance dogs and with first responders with mental issues. I have volunteered overseas, in Mexico, Timor-Leste and Vanuatu and with First Nations Indigenous communities. I began running half marathons at fifty-two years of age. I don't want my brain and body to stop operating – to me, age is just two numbers put together and it's about embracing where you are in the world. I feel like I'm in my early adult years with a far better understanding of who I am and with more adventure in my life! With a fire burning bright, I've managed to turn my pain into my purpose and passion!

I remarried and believe that love is spelt R-I-S-K – as if you don't take a risk, you will never know what is possible. As someone who has built a life around assessing risk, in comparison to the benefit, the risk of love is probably worth it!

This is the next story I want written for women ...

I want women to have a community and share their journeys and stories, their wins and losses, to find out who they are and believe in themselves well before they are fifty. We teach kids academia and not life skills, nor do we have them sit with community elders. I would like to see women like bowerbirds – gathering, sharing and creating our nests together, learning from older generations. I believe in human rights and us all understanding each other, returning to our basics in sitting, talking and listening.

I want women to be their own hero, their own legend and to create something that they will be remembered by. We are each our own most important person in life, and we need to be well physically, mentally and emotionally to be a better version of ourselves today than yesterday.

This is the next story I am writing for myself ...

My next story is to keep learning new things and being open-minded to the direction that my life will take. When I see the opportunity and next steps forward, I will seize the day. I will continue to dream big and see each day as an adventure where I learn something new. I have seen a lot of trauma and understand the fragility of life. In a split second everything can change. All we have is moments.

I want this piece, my life and story to this date to be a message of hope. Hope that no matter what you have been through in life, there is a way through and a light that is waiting for you. And remember, 'thriving, not just surviving' comes from a place of wellness, and from this place, we become our biggest contributors to ourselves, the people around us and our local and global communities.

Camille R Francis

41 | From: St Catherine, Jamaica | Lives: Maryland, USA

The act of giving replenishes my soul because I do it out of love and it serves the greater good of humanity. Love out the hate!

This is who I am in the world ...

I'm a global youth advocate who has volunteered over ten thousand hours serving youth from low- to moderate-income families in the US and around the world. This was a collaborative effort through my partnership with community organisations, Parent Teacher Student Associations, the National Association for the Advancement of Colored People, my church – Crossfire Worship Centre – my past and present employers and Junior Achievement. My passion for quality education, entrepreneurship, work preparedness, equality and social justice stems from multiple factors.

The foundation of who I am as a woman, mother, daughter, sister and friend is my faith in Jesus Christ. I am inspired by a quote from my favourite book which says, 'Faith without works is dead.' As a believer, my faith pushes me forward to serve and make a difference in the life of others. At ten years old I gave my heart to the Lord and was baptised, a decision that would revolutionise my thinking and life forever. I come from a lineage of elders who were founding members of the Methodist and Apostolic churches in St Ann's Bay, Jamaica – a legacy I am grateful for. The truths in the good book have guided me on how to live and thrive, and so can you!

The second and third factors are my parents who were instrumental in helping to shape my identity. I was raised by a Jamaican dad who was a police officer and lover of self-development books. He often encouraged me to study the dictionary and read books that would challenge my thinking around social justice. My Cuban mom, a seamstress by trade, wore many hats, one of which was an entrepreneur and translator for the ambassador of Argentina in Jamaica. After my parents divorced, I recalled that my mom would do anything to ensure that my sisters and I had what we needed. I found it kind of poetic watching her in the art of negotiation. My mom could sell anything from figurines to chicken. I admired her strength and courage. I'm eternally grateful for the values they have instilled in me and my work ethic. Glean from the wisdom of those that came before you.

According to the National Crime Victimization Survey, one out of every six American women has been the victim of an attempted or completed rape in her lifetime. This leads me to the fourth factor that has shaped my passion. At the age of twelve, I was gang-raped. I kept it secret from my parents until I was nineteen. The burden of carrying such trauma was unbearable and affected me in more ways than one. I had internalised the abuse which made it seem like it was happening to me over and over again. Through counselling, much prayer, seeking the support I needed and sharing my story, it allowed me not to stay depressed. I felt broken. I know what it's like to feel trapped in your own mind. I'm so grateful that I didn't let my circumstance and fear overtake me. I resolved to rise up and own my story since it had shaped me into the woman that I am. I know that my rape story would liberate over a billion women and girls in the future to come. As well as boys and men who are victimised, which is not discussed as much. It was worth the risk of sharing my story instead of living with regret and shame. Be strong and courageous and share your story!

The fifth factor was being bullied in high school as a student from a foreign country. According to the National Center for Education Statistics in 2019, one in five students reported being bullied at school. When I was sixteen years old, I migrated to the US for my sophomore year of high school. I was bullied in the hallway and classroom for my Jamaican accent and the clothes I wore, which were nice to me but not the trendy type to my critics. I started having anxiety attacks before going to school every morning and truly dreaded the name-calling and insults which happened repeatedly. Things changed after my dad visited the school multiple times to advocate on my behalf and to support me through my concerns.

Additionally, I tested out of my regular classes and was moved for the most part to honours classes. This change motivated me to get involved and give back to my local community and school by joining the Spanish club, the track team, honour societies, making new friends and tutoring students in the library. The bullying eventually stopped. I realised that the students that were picking on me were doing so because they lacked something, and I forgave them for how I was treated and showed them love instead. By giving back, I watched the attitudes of a lot of my bullies turn around. I chose to love out the hate, hurt and pain that they had caused me. Love out the hate!

This is the next story I want written for women ...

I want women to be strong and courageous despite the challenges that they'll face in the present and future and to seek the help they need from those who have hurt them so that healing can take place in their hearts, minds and soul and to love those that caused the offence anyway and move forward from the pain. If it's possible, learn to live peacefully with everyone and pursue peace in all your endeavours. Your story is impactful and worth the risk of sharing as you will liberate others instead of living with regret and shame.

This is the next story I am writing for myself ...

I am aware of my power now and reflect on the many opportunities missed where I could have used my voice to save a woman's life. I've decided to be brave TODAY. Every day, I consciously choose to not cower but to be BRAVE. My children are watching – my family, my community and the world is watching. When I walk in my power, it empowers others to walk in theirs. I choose to love out the hate, hurt and pain in the world. This act of love is my legacy. I'm passionate about giving as it replenishes my soul and serves the greater good of humanity. Our power grows when it is shared. Love out the hate!

Ambra Cristaldi

39 | From: Sicily, Italy | Lives: Malta

We are not made just to generate life, but also to accompany what is already existing in this world with the most caring, gentle, and yet solid presence.

This is who I am in the world …

My greatest passion is to live. I want to grab life and bite it until the very end.

As a child, my mom instilled in me a strong sense of independence, empowerment, hard work and constant improvement. My father taught me humbleness, sacrifice and commitment. Therefore, by the age of twenty-three, I became an engineer and moved out of the tiny village I grew up in (barely five thousand inhabitants near Mount Etna), away from my beloved family, friends and comfort zone.

Exactly as I always imagined as a child, I became a determined, independent, successful woman who was living her life at her best. I easily married the love of my life at the age of twenty-six, and my last step to fulfil the 'perfect life plan' was to become a mother.

Little did I know about the struggle I would go through to achieve that.

I always loved children; becoming a mother was meant to be the greatest thing in life, yet it broke me into a million pieces.

Firstly, I had one ovary and one tube removed, and I never felt less of a woman than in that period.

Secondly, I had multiple miscarriages and I felt I just couldn't carry a child.

Finally, when my girls were born, I made the mistake of thinking that it would be like shown in the media: you give birth and the next day you are out looking beautiful, almost celestial, ready for a photo shoot holding your baby angel.

I even chose a natural birth with no painkillers ('like a billion women in history had done!'), because I wanted to 'feel alive through it', stitches and all … Why do I have to be so stubborn sometimes? I felt completely ashamed when, a few days after delivery, I peed my pants!

So, basically, this was my motherhood: I had no clue how to deal with a baby, my nipples were hurting, I looked like crap and I was not in control anymore.

To be honest, when my first daughter Morena was born and I held her in my arms for the first time, I couldn't cry. I was just staring at her, contemplating her perfection – I even counted her fingers!

Suddenly, I realised that my life as I used to know it till that moment didn't exist anymore.

They tell us that a mother falls in love with her kid the instant the pregnancy test is positive. Well, I can tell you this is not always the case. Sometimes, it's a gradual process to learn how to deal with the new person you're requested to be and a new little human who suddenly depends on you.

I had just become familiar with my new routine when I found myself a mother again. Just over a year later, Morena's sister Clara was born. She came into this world through a C-section, so no 'primitive hero mother' this time, which contributed to making me feel unworthy and unfitting again.

It was not a question of how much I loved my baby girls, but myself. I remember this as the toughest period of my life, mostly filled with loneliness.

In my mind, *I was failing*.

This dragging feeling of failure, I think, is what made my first years of motherhood emotionally precarious, feeling as though I was in the eye of a hurricane and observing the world spinning around me.

It was through the strong presence of my precious husband, Alessio, and my amazing sister, Alice, that I came out of it. Sometimes, awakening can take the shape of an email sent by your sister, where she shows you the image she has of you and asks you to wake up.

It was like a slap in the face, and I came back.

Not an easy journey, but I eventually made peace with this new version of me and accepted my own evolution as cathartic.

When my third daughter, Aurora, was born a few years later, I was ready for it: a painful VBAC (again, what's wrong with me and this need to constantly feel alive?) but worth every second. I cried when I held her for the first time.

Maternity, finally, became the most amazing thing I'd done in my life.

This is the next story I want written for women …

It is not a secret that I stand for women. We can adjust to changes and circumstances in the most resilient ways, and we are incredible at self-determination.

However, we are not made *just* to generate life, but also to accompany what is already existing in this world with the most caring, gentle and yet solid presence.

Motherhood doesn't have to be a task to accomplish and especially not the sole meaning of life and happiness.

Our self-actualisation has to happen as human beings first.

Today, I have three precious young girls who are intelligent, caring, conscious about the world, sensitive and beautiful. I try to teach them what I wish for all women in the world: to be smart, independent, to have dreams and chase them, to be kind and especially to always love themselves for who they truly are. Embracing our limits is the first step towards a more balanced life journey. I wish they will fight for what they aim to achieve and never passively listen to anyone who will try to undermine them or to convince them that 'you can't'. Instead, use criticism in a constructive way and to make sure they have knowledge and compassion, mind and heart as the most powerful weapons they could ever use.

This is the next story I am writing for myself …

I would be lying if I didn't say this is what I wish for myself too. To continue being a strong but caring human being, chasing opportunities, looking for new challenges, seeking motivation in the difficult moments and actualising myself through my daily life experiences.

I wish to wake up every morning and have the courage to cross out items from my long bucket list of life accomplishments. And I truly never gave up on that project to travel around the world on a Harley Davidson with my husband one day.

Needless to say, I will sit in the driver's seat.

Komal Kaur

37 | From: Singapore | Lives: Bali, Indonesia

I envision a world where women are so beautifully connected to their minds, emotions and bodies, and have all the tools necessary to counteract stressful events, so that they don't get left behind with trauma and fear.

This is who I am in the world ...

I am a woman. DNA and imaginary lines drawn on a map would identify me as Indian-Singaporean.

I am a student of my life experiences. I am a keeper and a proliferator of the wisdom gained from these experiences.

I am a philosopher, storyteller and psychic.

I am a practitioner of sungazing, qi gong and meditation.

I soothe people's nervous systems with vibrational medicine using psychedelic hypnagogic lights and singing bowls.

I am a physical body with a logically functioning brain that perceives every feeling and emotion as deeply as if my senses were on steroids.

I am a daughter, a sister, an ex-wife and a lover.

I am a mother of four rescued fur babies and the sponsor of a child saved from a miserable childhood of breaking stones in a Ugandan stone quarry.

I am an ex-child-member of an international Japanese cult. I was initiated at an age when I had no agency over my life's choices. After gaining eight years of age, critical thinking skills and subsequently courage to 'rebel', I refused to participate any longer and was the first of several family members to leave.

I am a wayshower.

I am a Sikh, and I am a trauma survivor.

I am a dancer, an artist(e) and a singer. I have performed publicly for thousands and privately for no-one.

I am a biotechnologist turned digital nomad who left my 'safe' life behind for love, lived out of a suitcase and travelled around the world to over forty countries in seven years.

I am perfectly imperfect.

I am all these labels, and I am none of them.

I am a reinventor of myself.

And I am here to show other women how to break their shackles.

The shackles that get locked tightly on us in childhood, and which only get tighter as we age. The unforgiving and painful shackles of parental and societal conditioning, of our mind's limiting beliefs, of fear and trauma.

In the past, internal/external conflicts would create stress, an insidious force that impacted many areas of my wellbeing. I didn't even notice or deal with it because my system and society had normalised operating under pressure.

I am here to encourage women to embrace rest as a necessary tool in self-care and stress relief using the healing frequencies of sound and light technology. I add intuitive reflections to gently guide women to reconnect to their inner truth and voice of intuition, becoming their own inspired guides.

I am here to empower women to fully express their voice out into the world. Without shame, without guilt, without fear.

But first, let's address the important question:

What is the world?

Well, is it not simply an echo chamber of our preconditioned belief systems?

A brilliantly organised construct that only mirrors back to us the truth of our inner world?

That is what I believe.

Therefore, 'who I am in the world' continues to evolve.

And the world evolves with me.

This is the next story that I want written for women ...
Dear sister,

I envision a world that feels safe for you. For all parts of you.

From birth, to death.

In this 'go-go-go' programmed world, I want you to give yourself permission to rest.

To slow down. To honour your body, your feelings, your emotions.

Just as our muscles cannot grow without targeted stress, spirit invites challenges into our lives for our spiritual growth.

We are custodians of the world, nourishing generations with our love and resolute strength. But overwhelming stress diminishes our light.

Stress is a major contributing factor for all the leading causes of premature death, and I want us to develop a healthy relationship to it.

I envision a world where women are so beautifully connected to their minds, emotions and bodies, and have all the tools necessary to counteract stressful events, that they don't get left behind with trauma and fear. We can heal and transform our lives!

I want to inspire women to dedicate one day a week to their self-care.

Mondays are my non-negotiable self-care day. Depending on how I feel (yes, we are dynamic beings, and we can honour that) I laze in bed or go for a sunrise walk on the beach. I might schedule a beauty treatment. Maybe I will have a quiet evening and run a divine Epsom salt bath with essential oils.

I have a list of all the things that bring me pleasure. And I want every woman to have her own 'pleasure list'.

When I found myself alone in an unfamiliar town in the global pandemic, after leaving an eleven-year relationship with a man I wanted to grow old with, I created my 'pleasure list'. I prioritised therapy and self-care. I gave myself the love and comfort I craved and missed from my partner. I turned my pain into power.

Your peaceful and calm state of mind is non-negotiable. Hitting the system reset button on stress on a consistent basis is non-negotiable.

Nourish yourself. Bring softness back into your heart for yourself. Use kinder words when talking about yourself.

And when we come back to our individual points of power, to our personal zones of genius, I invite you to step out into the world and collaborate with other women that match your frequency.

Collaborate, not compete.

Like this book of fifty-five women, together, weaving a story more powerful than the individual.

Because, together, we rise.

This is the next story I am writing for myself ...

I'm writing a story in which I am a wayshower.

In which I continue to step into my fears, see 'failures' as vital learning lessons and keep unveiling and unlocking more shackles that keep my spirit small.

I will marry science with spirit. Technology with ancient healing techniques.

The world will reflect on me the infinite love, collaborative flow states and highest potential I envision for all of us.

In my story, I will arrive at my final beautiful breaths on this earth, look back at my life and feel a sense of peace with all my decisions.

And I want each breath, from this moment until my last, to be the most unapologetic expression of ME.

Erin Cotter-Smith

46 | Lives: Melbourne, Australia

I want to see a growing awareness of how trauma is the invisible force that shapes our lives. It shapes the way we live, the way we love and the way we make sense of the world.

This is who I am in the world ...

In 2005, I met a woman who would change my life. With a mass of long black curls, she had a warm smile and a laugh like sunshine, but her dark eyes were a window to past trauma. As we sat in a cafe across from a firehouse in New York, Marian Fontana shared with me the story of her firefighter husband Dave who had died in the South Tower of the World Trade Center on 9/11.

A stand-up comedian before the terrorist attacks, Marian had a unique gift of finding moments of humour in her story of heart-breaking loss; at times I wasn't sure if the tears leaking from my eyes were from sadness or laughter. By the time we finished our coffee across from Dave's firehouse, I knew two things unequivocally: I wanted to be her friend, and I wanted to learn more about the stories of the 9/11 first responders who ran towards the burning buildings when everyone else ran out.

It's funny how things turn out. Marian is now one of my most treasured friends, and since 2005 I have shared the stories of hundreds of 9/11 first responders. They have invited me into their homes, into their memories, into their nightmares. They have opened vacuum-sealed bags letting putrid air escape, revealing dusty uniforms, boots and helmets.

Sometimes the words don't come, tears silently falling. When the words do arrive, they are richly descriptive and deeply personal, offering a powerful reminder that the story of 9/11 did not end when the towers fell.

I may not have been there, but I can tell you what it smelled like. I can tell you what it looked like. I can tell you what it sounded like. I can tell you because I have listened. For nearly two decades I have been the secret keeper, which is an incredible honour.

At some point though, the stories seeped in. Was that their nightmare that just woke me at 3am, or mine? Where do I safely hold these stories? These secrets? On sleepless nights I would lay awake trying to exorcise other people's demons, plagued by moments of violence and destruction that I had not directly witnessed.

By the time I recognised my vicarious trauma I was already years into my nightmares, intrusive thoughts, deep sadness and anxiety. The more I had been invited into their homes, connected with their families and entrusted with their secrets, the more I too became psychologically scarred by the terrorist attacks.

When a plane flew low and loud overhead I would look towards the sky in fear. When an elevator opened in a high-rise building, I would imagine people in flames running out, their screams filling the lobby. When I closed my eyes, I would see myself buried in the piles of burning rubble and twisted metal.

But along with the trauma has come an incredible opportunity for growth. I now share not only the stories of others, but my own story of vicarious trauma, PTSD and lived experience.

This is the next story I want written for women ...

As someone who has dedicated my life to sharing stories of survival and trauma, I want to see a growing awareness of how trauma is the invisible force that shapes our lives. It shapes the way we live, the way we love and the way we make sense of the world. It is often the root of our deepest wounds, but it can also be the source of our most profound self-awareness and growth.

I used to believe that trauma was caused by 'bad things' happening to people: like disaster, war, murder and violence. What I have learned since 9/11 is that trauma happens to everybody, in deeply personal and complex ways. Individually and collectively, we carry a cumulation of pain that has never been heard because we lack safe narratives to help us share, witness and hold space for each other's deepest wounds.

The story I want written for women is one where we all feel psychologically safe enough to walk down the path of healing.

This is the next story I am writing for myself …

I recently stood at the water's edge with a dear friend. We had been sharing our thoughts and reflections on where we were in our lives and of the traumas that had helped shape us. In a sudden move, my friend took out her phone and threw it into the waves that were gently lapping at our feet. 'What did you just do?' I cried out! 'Liberate myself,' she replied.

It was a powerful moment; for her it symbolised her need to stop being so responsive to the world around her. The constant demands from work, family, friends. 'Do it!' She encouraged me. 'You need to stop sharing everyone else's stories and focus on your own.' It was true, I had spent so much of the last twenty years sharing the stories of others that somewhere along the way I had forgotten my own.

But the thought of throwing my phone into the ocean filled me with anxiety. I slowly stepped back out of the cool water and sat and reflected on the ways I could start focusing on my own story and heal from my own trauma.

So, what is the story I am now writing for myself? It's one of post-traumatic growth. It's one of continued healing and recovery. But most of all, it's one of self-awareness. I am finally choosing me!

Nadia Pace

42 | From: Malta | Lives: Malta

I often find myself the only woman in a boardroom. Was it daunting at first? Definitely! Did I feel I wanted to give up and go onto a different path? Many times! But I am here, and although I have come to grips with it, I would like to have other women join me here.

This is who I am in the world ...

Following my studies in commerce, I took up roles in business development within commercial settings. I left my safe, sheltered home country of Malta to live in Greece, where I led the development of a language school in Cyprus and other roles in Thessaloniki. Sitting on that plane and feeling exhilarated at the thought of new and exciting prospects and the possibility of growth – for me as a person and also as a woman at work – was quite a leap of faith.

I possess a sense of openness, and this adventure helped spark a further sense of learning. Besides being a picturesque country, Greece helped me interact with a different business culture – an experience I carry with me, particularly now that I have clients all over Europe.

It was a time when I was pushed far out of my comfort zone in terms of building relationships with people I had never met before – from different backgrounds, work ethics and ways of approaching things. I knew I had to start from the basics, and I made it a point to learn the language. Whilst I always enjoyed interacting with others, I was still developing my sense of self, and consequently, self-esteem was a work in progress. I still go back to Greece to relive that exhilarating sense of Mediterranean freedom and growth.

My family drew me back to Malta, where I worked with a customer service provider setting up the business development department beyond local shores. At thirty-four, my passion for growth led me to become the CEO. It came with its fair share of challenges – both from a business angle and when dealing with a myriad of characters. Nonetheless, it helped me grow and ingrained in me a sense of resilience.

It's now been four years since I've set up my own business consultancy, which focuses specifically on business advisory, mentoring and board directorships. I sit on boards as a non-executive director and advise businesses depending on their strategic vision and market of operation. Mind you, it is still immensely challenging, yet I feel empowered and am pleased to be working hand in hand with many men and women who embrace all that it is to be an assertive female. I am extremely thankful to all the bosses who believed in my abilities and supported me throughout my journey.

My intention was always to grow and learn through new experiences. Companies are made of teams which are ultimately made up of individuals that would require personal growth but also to grow and develop as a unit – as a team. To make business sense and for things to work in symphony, this growth must be in alignment with the company or business objectives.

I am reading a very interesting book, *Breaking the Habit of Being Yourself: How to Lose Your Mind and Create a New One* by Dr Joe Dispenza, which highlights how repeatedly taking the same decisions and practising the same routines will impede personal growth because as the saying goes 'if nothing changes, all stays the same'.

I want to empower women. I come across many women, in different parts of organisations and society, who have great potential, yet for some reason or other – either due to family commitments or societal preconceptions – refrain from pushing themselves within the realm of work. As women, we tend to second-guess ourselves, to overthink as we are more cautious than our male counterparts.

I want to leave an impact on the world and be seen and remembered as the woman who helped other women achieve. If women truly support one another, the sky's the limit.

This is the next story I want written for women …

Growing up, I was given the impression that the business world was a realm solely reserved for men – or better still 'masculinity', 'assertiveness', devoid of emotions the world often attributes to being female, such as 'compassion' and 'sensitivity'. I was also told that it is difficult to penetrate the business world as a woman unless you came from a line of business owners.

I often got the feeling that, since I was a woman, my opinion in business meetings was not given as much weight as that of a man, and the expression of emotions was often confused with panic, 'being hormonal' or the inability to handle the task at hand.

But I often now find myself the only woman in a boardroom. Was it daunting at first? Definitely! Did I feel I wanted to give up and go onto a different path? Many times! But I am here, and although I have gotten to grips with it, I would like to have other women join me here. Well, I guess I could do with more variety in the boardroom.

I encourage all women, far and wide, to set their femininity to good use. To trust their gut, to go for it and keep up the momentum whilst drawing clear boundaries between work and play. Let us show the world how to work hard, play fair and work to win. In a world which advocates for the importance of emotional intelligence, we do not need to disguise our emotions.

No matter where you're from, who your family is, if you set your mind to develop your skills, to enable yourself to achieve in whatever sector or life – you can do it. However, you need to allow yourself to achieve. To enable yourself to be the best version of yourself, wherever you are. It all starts with a positive mindset, and if this is achieved, maximising your strengths, opportunities and capabilities will follow.

This is the next story I am writing for myself ...

My consultancy business has grown in recent years. I have helped individuals, teams and companies explore different ways of doing things and grow beyond their boundaries and objectives. Yet, I'd like to hone into the female potential. As women, we are capable of handling so many things simultaneously, to work through ethics and respect. So, I'd like to keep cultivating this mentality and to push women beyond their potential, to stop second-guessing themselves and just take the leap.

Trudy Morter

38 | From: Melbourne, Australia | Lives: Melbourne, Australia

My next story is my initiation into motherhood and the learnings that come with being completely responsible for another human and offering them the care and wisdom to help them to grow into the best version of themselves.

This is who I am in the world ...

I am a sister, an aunt, a daughter, a friend and a soon-to-be mumma to a beautiful little girl.

I am also a kinesiologist, which means that I work with people's muscles to clear blocked energy. I specialise with people who are experiencing emotional and psychological challenges.

My current story is all about becoming a mumma and fulfilling this identity. I have a strong desire to learn about these aspects of myself and share this journey with another brave soul and pass on wisdom I have gained. The reason we are on this earth, other than to evolve, is to connect with others. I see no greater connection than bringing a little human earthside who is part of me and to form a bond and love like no other, selflessly devoting my time, space and energy to their evolution. I am ready to experience the joy, wonders and challenges of this chapter, bringing one of the greatest and biggest challenges in my life. I will be bent and stretched as far as I have ever known, and I am looking forward to meeting my edges in this way, experiencing the unconditional love and heart opening that people talk about.

I am a woman who has struggled to bring children into this world and surrendered to the fact that this may not be my reality in this lifetime. I have always had a deep, burning desire to birth children since I was a little girl. I used to babysit the kids in the neighbourhood and play mother, taking in many people over the years. The mother role is one I feel a closeness and familiarity with. It feels natural. It's a part of my identity that's deep within my bones, yearning to be expressed. To be felt. To be nurtured. To be loved. My divine feminine is awakening from the depths ready to play this cherished role.

At thirty-six, I separated from my boyfriend. I had this really strong calling to get my fertility checked and possibly freeze some eggs. I certainly wasn't getting any younger. A grim reality set in. I found out I had a benign tumour on my pituitary gland that had affected my hormones and fertility. I had a very low egg count for a woman my age. I was told that if I didn't have children within a year, that would be it. My world felt like it had come crashing down. With strong masculine energy, I'm not a procrastinator so I went into action mode. I knew that becoming a mother was something I HAD to do. I made the decision to take this journey alone.

I got a donor, started my journey with IVF and made a decision to turn my health around. This was to regulate my hormonal system and naturally reduce my tumour. I went on a massive internal journey. I went on a plant-based diet and was seeing my kinesiologist regularly. I started exercising more, attending yoga and Pilates daily. I saw an acupuncturist. I meditated. I started taking supplements recommended by a fertility specialist naturopath. I went on plant medicine journeys, attending retreats to clear up past trauma and to also meet my edges. I was committed.

Over a year of doing IVF later, my follicle count had improved; however, it took a toll on me mentally, emotionally and financially. I decided to take a break and to just live life while I figured out my next move.

After three months, a very dear friend contacted me and said they could not sit by and watch me not have children, offering to be an anonymous donor. We discussed what it would mean for us both individually and how it would work. I excitedly said yes, and we got started right away. With the first try, I fell pregnant. As I write this, I'm currently seventeen weeks pregnant.

My most pivotal moment was when I saw the positive line on the test and realised I'm going to be a mumma. The second was the twelve-week mark when I went for the ultrasound and saw my little bubba moving and heard her heartbeat. I have since settled and realised that this is real. I have had a gender reveal, celebrated with close family and friends and have started making preparations to welcome my beautiful little girl into my home, my heart and my life.

I will always remember this moment as beautiful and appreciate how blessed and eternally grateful I am. My first twelve weeks were a huge adjustment as I held hope with no guarantees. It has been a roller-coaster of emotions: elation, joy, bliss, magic, belief and honour. At other times I have felt very deeply alone on this solo journey, remembering that I am in fact surrounded by much love from some really beautiful people.

This is the next story I want written for women ...

As a woman who wants to have children, don't give up on your dreams. There is a way. I had beautiful women offer to donate their eggs, and I seriously considered it. There are Facebook groups with donors, and in Australia, you can use your superannuation to make it affordable. There is surrogacy. Adoption. There are many options. Infertility is real and it's more common than we think. The road can be scary, however, if it's something you truly want, there will be a way. Keep looking!

This is the next story I am writing for myself ...

My next story is my initiation into motherhood and blossoming like a flower in springtime. I can feel myself glowing from the inside out. I am ready for the learnings that come with being responsible for another human and offering them care, love and wisdom to help them to grow into the best possible version of themselves. I am devoted to this journey.

I am also passionate about helping others who are embarking on their fertility journey. I have been through the wash a few times, and I would love to help other people find their shine, using kinesiology with others trying to fall pregnant, during and post-birth.

Michelle Poole

49 | From: Wisconsin, USA | Lives: Green Bay, Wisconsin, USA

My story is to continue to improve myself while reaching back around and pulling others forward.

This is who I am in the world ...

I am an entrepreneur who has found my purpose while healing childhood trauma.

I was always told I was shy and quiet growing up, and this is how friends and family would describe me. For the most part, that description is accurate. I was quiet and not very outgoing around people I didn't know well and larger groups of people. This wasn't because I didn't like people or didn't want to be there, it was because I was too preoccupied scanning the room for people that might seem unsafe or sketchy. I only trusted my parents and siblings not to hurt me. I was hypervigilant. I had my guard up around people all the time.

I was carrying a terrible secret. I was being sexually abused by a family relative since the age of six. At least, that is the earliest I can remember it. I didn't tell anyone until I was sixteen. In my sophomore year of high school, I told my best friend. At the time, I had to tell another living soul as I thought I was going to burst if I didn't. My anxiety was through the roof. Dating was completely out of the question, as just the thought of going on a date made me feel physically ill.

As I entered my early twenties, I began going out with friends to bars. I found partying and drinking suppressed how I had been feeling my whole life up until that point. I didn't realise that I was suppressing what had happened rather than dealing with it.

I married at the age of thirty and had my first child at thirty-two, and the trauma and associated feelings came roaring back! I knew how to protect myself in the world, yet how do I protect this little child?! I had my second child at thirty-six. The anxiety of being a mother was overwhelming and I knew I needed help. I knew I had to release and start healing the impact of the trauma I had been carrying since childhood. I was tense all the time and I was never really happy. I rarely smiled and I couldn't continue like this.

I tried talk therapy when I was about twenty, but it didn't work for me. I didn't get the results I hoped for, yet I couldn't continue as I was. I could feel the physical effects of carrying the trauma and the secret on my body. I was tired, my lower back was always sore and my shoulders and neck were tight. This wasn't how I wanted to live. My past was affecting my present and would affect my future if I didn't do something. I was desperate and determined to get out of this prison.

I knew there was so much more that was waiting for me, and I wanted – I needed – to grab on to whatever it was with both hands. I prayed a lot, and I cried a lot when I prayed. I asked God to lead me in the right direction to heal. I made a deal with God, if that is even possible. If he would bring me through this, I would spend the rest of my life helping others heal and move forward as well.

I knew that God was listening when I was introduced to energy sound therapy seven years ago. I was at the end of my rope, hanging on to the knotted end with one hand. Energy sound therapy brought me back. It was my lifeline and a gateway to a brand-new life.

This is the next story I want written for women ...

I want every woman to tell their stories, not just for themselves, but for others. As a child, I thought I was the only one who was abused. I felt like a freak, weird, not normal and somehow damaged in a way I couldn't escape from. I felt very alone. I felt I couldn't tell anyone. I planned on taking this secret to my grave because I felt nobody would believe me, especially because of who my abuser was. He was practically revered in my family.

Now, I realise through my energy sound therapy business, I have a lot of company in this area. Women of all ages have come to me for help. Before they even sit down in my office and the door is closed, they are crying. It is time to release what isn't ours and send it back to the appropriate owner and heal ourselves so we can move forward as our best selves.

I would like to see women take the time to inventory their life from childhood to the present. What are your carrying that isn't yours that is affecting you today? What programming are you still running that isn't true? Programming that you accepted because you gave your power away. Stepping into that reflective state can be both frightening and empowering.

Shedding the beliefs that were handed down to us and releasing the experiences from our past that may be holding us back can feel like floating back to the surface and coming up for air.

That first breath is amazing!

This is the next story I am writing for myself ...

Healing from trauma has truly been a journey for me and continues to be. I look at how far I have come and I am amazed. I can now talk about my experience and share it with others and how it affected me. I continue to use my current tools to further my healing.

I have an amazing circle of friends to lean on when needed who also use holistic approaches. I continue to add to my knowledge and toolset to expand on helping myself and others.

I like to think that God took me up on the deal I offered him. I plan on holding up my end. My story is to continue to improve myself while reaching back and pulling others forward.

Mary Deng-Crisp

26 | From: South Sudan | Lives: Melbourne, Australia

We're capable of bringing life into the world, but we've been conditioned to settle for far less than we are worth.

This is who I am in the world ...

I am compassionate, loyal and unbelievably tenacious.

I am fierce and always learning.

My name is Mary, and I was born in a small village in South Sudan. I moved to Australia in 2005 and completed my schooling here.

Throughout my life, I have always been surrounded by incredibly strong women. From my birth mother to adoptive mother, girlfriends, female colleagues and aunties. I have always believed that I could achieve whatever I wanted so long as I was willing to work hard, and I watched these women lead by example. They don't always get it right, but I think true strengths lie in our ability to always be learning and evolving as people and an acceptance of the fact that, as humans, we're not faultless, and learning is such a beautiful part of it all.

I graduated with a Bachelor of Social Sciences and recently completed my honours in psychological sciences. I currently work as a family violence practitioner, working with perpetrators of family violence. In my nine-to-five role, I assess risk and work with adult men who use violence, in an attempt to include them in the conversation of gendered violence and keep them in focus, whilst holding them accountable. I also work with victims and survivors of family violence, primarily women and children, some nights and weekends.

The juxtaposition of the two roles is very interesting. I am passionate about working with people who use violence in general, particularly those in the forensic system. I think that people are capable of incredible things under the right conditions, and I want to be involved in how we can rewrite the narrative with men who use violence. I want to know how we can utilise what we already know about fear and trauma responses to educate and hold men accountable for their choices and take responsibility for their behaviours.

In the case for people who perpetrate family violence, I love that I get to have an opportunity to talk with them, learn their (trauma) history, watch them be vulnerable in a way that is usually not acceptable in our society, and for some, watch them embark on this journey of healing. I think we live in a society where men are conditioned to not be vulnerable and are celebrated for being 'manly and tough'. I love that in my role I get to expose that myth and challenge men to think beyond 'it's what I was taught' and watch them begin to develop those introspective skills. I firmly believe that to fix a problem, you must start at the source – and in this case, gendered violence is predominately perpetrated by men, so I believe that working with men to address this is very important.

I also love that I get to interact with those impacted by family violence. It is both heartbreaking and incredibly humbling to watch women not just survive incredibly traumatic and horrendous things done to them by people who are meant to represent safety and calmness, but to hear their stories and watch them try to rebuild, to trust again, despite it all, is unbelievably inspiring.

This is the next story I want written for women ...

The next story I want written for women is one that they get to write themselves. I think for far too long society has had this crazy expectation that things need to be done for women, to a point where it has become a symbol of weakness. I want to change this narrative that women need to be taken care of and show that women are more than capable of having 100% authorship over their own destinies, whatever that may look like.

One of my absolute pet peeves is witnessing injustice and feeling like I can't do anything about it. I personally believe that there is something fundamentally evil about people not being afforded their own free will and allowed to make basic choices. I understand that it's idealistic, but it's this belief that motivates me to do what I do. To be honest, I think a part of this stems from my own upbringing and wanting the opposite of what I had growing up. My formative years were very chaotic, and I felt like I had very little choice in what my environment looked like. It took a lot of internal work to get to a point where I was not questioning every move I made as a free-thinking adult. I am very much still a work in progress but I'm learning to be content with how the story unfolds.

Women are powerful and not just in the 'I'm a strong independent woman' mantra-type way, but in the truest sense of the word. As women, the odds are against us, in general, from the very beginning. You add in other variables, like belonging to a minority group, and the stakes get higher, yet we thrive in spite of all that. I believe that as women, we have so much more power than we're conditioned to accept. We're capable of bringing life into the world but we've been conditioned to settle for far less than we are worth. We're taught to accept the bare minimum and be thankful for the little things. The next story I want written for women is one where it is the norm for women to simply be 'bosses' and not *'girl* bosses' or 'prime minister' and not *female* prime minister'. To say 'no' without fear of repercussions, to have a family and be the CEO without their capability questioned, to come home to a consistently safe environment and to simply exist without consequences.

This is the next story I am writing for myself ...

What I want next for myself, others might consider to be mundane, but I want consistency and stability. I love working nine to five and the consistency that comes with it. I want to contain my chaos into a form that is manageable so that it doesn't consume me. I want to be content. I want peace. This is where creativity, for me, can be funnelled into one singular point and I can be the most useful in my work and life.

Bianca Raby

38 | From: Adelaide, Australia | Lives: Canggu, Bali

I want to see women forgive the masculine. I want to see women forgive each other.

This is who I am in the world ...

First and foremost, I am a sovereign being doing my best to flow with what this life offers me. I am committed to my own personal development and strive to show up as the best version of myself.

Born with a desire to learn, transform and guide others, I identify as an educator. Everything that I have created stems from a place of growth and a desire to inspire those around me.

Other labels used to describe my personal imprint on society include: CEO, founder, entrepreneur, teacher, writer, creator, author, producer and leader.

Personally, I am an 'ex' to a string of men, a best friend to a few, a good friend to more, an aunty, an almost-mother, a daughter, a sister, and most importantly, a woman with an incredible capacity to love.

There was an easy path laid out for me. I could have chosen a quiet and predictable life. But the soul wants what the soul wants, and so I played my joker card at twenty-five and switched lanes. This meant starting a relatively new life as a single woman in London. Searching for clues as to who I actually was without a man. What would I choose for myself if spared the influence of others?

Already 'wise beyond my years' according to all adults around me, divorcing at twenty-five certainly thrust me into 'adulting' with a vengeance. This was where I first encountered deep shame while at the same time feeling a tremendous burst of courage and trust in myself. I mean, it would have been easy to stay. We had a nice life full of 'stuff', routines and a cute bipolar cat.

Instead, I threw caution to the wind and spent ten years inside the washing machine of life. Bouncing around jobs, countries, projects and relationships. Falling in and out of love – learning a bit more about myself each time. Embracing the full extent of my Gemini-ness. Then, at thirty-five, I hit a level of emotional exhaustion I've never felt before. You know, that moment when you become fed up with yourself? Fed up with the life you supposedly created?

And so, I finally went inwards. To the depths, while in the mothering energy of Ubud, Bali. I quit drinking alcohol, cleaned up my diet, stayed home more, slept more and slowed the F down. I learned how to balance (or at least what to do to cultivate it). I saw signs of burnout early enough to hold it at bay. And most importantly, I found alignment in what I do every day to contribute to the world.

Today, I am proud to say I am on a nonstop journey of self-discovery and a quest to cultivate more and more trust in myself. I do this by engaging with everything life throws at me and seeking growth at every corner.

This is the next story I want written for women ...

There are many things I wish for women right now and for those who will come after me. Each stems from trust. Trust in our essence, trust in our bodies, trust in our intuition, trust in our path and trust in each other.

Too many generations have passed where the feminine has been dismissed, ridiculed, bullied or aggressively attacked from all corners of society. Then, as if to make matters worse, we have retaliated by attacking the masculine, blinded by the consequences of this.

Women have an enormous capacity for forgiveness and an innate resolve to love above all else. I wish for all women to understand this at their core and see it as the greatest strength they have. I wish all women courageously transform their traumas and the traumas of those before them, as this is how we will heal the planet.

I want to see women lead as women (not as women acting like men). I want to see women leading decision-making from a place of connection. I want to see women honouring their bodies. I want to see women forgive the masculine. I want to see women forgive each other.

I want us to forgive ourselves.

Once this is all 'in the bag', then I say we all ride off on unicorns into the sunset!

This is the next story I am writing for myself ...

My next chapter will be about love, relationships and motherhood. After dedicating so much of my adult life to pursuing a meaningful career, I crave a more balanced life. It's time.

I will never stop growing and creating; however, my next most significant challenge is to do this in a way that makes space for an equal, supportive partner to arrive. I so desperately want to trust the masculine. To really move into my true essence as a creator and nurturer of life.

I want so much more joy, play and adventure in my next chapter. I know how to be in the dark. I know how to be in the light. Now, I crave the freedom that comes from a strong sense of safety and inner knowing. As I approach my forties, I welcome a new air of confidence and a strong sense of self.

I want to treat my body as the temple that it is. I want to tame my mind. I want to be continuously and relentlessly curious. I want to own all the parts of me so that acceptance becomes a more natural state of mind.

And finally, I want to know how to surround myself with adorable cats but not be labelled as a 'crazy cat lady'!

Kylie L Clarke

47 | From: Penrith, New South Wales, Australia | Lives: Dungog, New South Wales, Australia

I am much more than just a woman. I am spirit, energy, love, and I am human.

This is who I am in the world ...

Truth? For a while, I forgot who I was in this world.

I *used* to be fierce, creative and confident. I *was* sure of my footing and extremely happily married in what I can only describe as a fairytale.

I was a very successful singer and performer, owning one of Australia's largest tribute acts, Th!nk Pink – The Ultimate Tribute. I worked alongside amazing humans who kept me working hard and reaching for a higher standard in myself.

I've never believed in starting at the bottom and working my way up. Ever. I've always run, jumped and grabbed onto the highest rung of the ladder that I can possibly reach, then held on white-knuckled as I quickly learned how to fit into that space, building my successful business, show and organisation from there.

Then, everything changed. The spotlights, self, what I thought my life was – over.

I lost twelve loved ones very quickly. My father, grandfather, both grandmothers, beautiful friends and the hardest of all, my lifelong friend of twenty-five years and loving wife of a short three and a half years.

My wife died at home with me by her side in May 2021, a short and fast eleven months after her diagnosis of stage four cancer. I was dismantled.

There is not a single thing in this existence as soul-destroying as watching the love of your life, the reason you smile every morning, slip away right in front of you.

The world slowed down around me and became silent as I watched my love take her last breath.

I was unwell during her last few months and required major abdominal surgery four days after her service.

By the time *my* healing journey began, I'd concluded that nothing meant anything anymore. I no longer wanted to sing, perform or continue my non-profit.

As I laid in bed for weeks recovering and mourning, a crazy little TV show took my interest. I read about its creator and its actors, passing time as I healed. This led me to learn about a non-profit one of the actors had built. A crack of inspiration crept in, and I felt what resembled hope. Soon after, I reimagined my entire organisation and it simultaneously began rebuilding me.

I rode a roller-coaster of emotions after my wife left. Smiling largely at the wonderful memories and hurting deeply over things I could never change. I began questioning everything.

I was very raw emotionally, so my answers were surprisingly honest and very confronting, leading me to have the most unbelievable realisations about myself, my childhood and the protection I didn't get from neglect, abuse and sexual interference. About how the self-concepts I developed from these experiences shaped how I showed up as an adult, and of course, how it all played a role in every single thing about myself. I had *finally* woken up.

So … Who am I in this world?

I am a forty-seven-year-old widowed, strong human raising two beautiful children on my own. I am also an authorised foster carer raising my voice for the children and carers often neglected by the fractured system that was designed to protect them.

I stay connected and grow through online communities and initiatives created by amazing souls that inspire me daily to never give up as I, too, work to create initiatives to help children and the people raising them – the world over.

I am the founding director of the non-profit charity Belamore House Ltd and the podcast *The Inside Out Of Me*.

I am a singer, songwriter, performer and screenwriter. I am a human who won't quit and is finding their way back. More importantly, I am you.

This is the next story I want written for all humans

I am much more than just a woman. I am spirit, energy, love, and I am human.

Like all humans, regardless of assigned birth gender or gender identification, what I want is to see a balance of respect and love so all humans can be the very best versions of themselves, without judgement from others and especially without judgement from themselves.

My awakening helped me out of repetitive trauma-related behaviour and into healing. I work to bring this awareness to other people.

Children go into statutory care because somewhere along the genealogy, a parent or caregiver encountered trauma, removing their capacity to safely parent. That statistically stems from their own experiences with perpetual abuse and/or neglect.

This familial pattern of emotional dysfunction revolves like an endless Stephen King evil carousel that ends badly, regardless of what lens is on it or how hard the main characters work to change the script. This breaks my fucking heart daily.

What would give my soul the greatest hope for humanity is to work towards strategies to greatly reduce the perpetual re-traumatisation of all humans.

Humans come with a very simple three-step manual:

To feel seen.

To feel heard.

To feel loved.

If we continue moving towards this, one beautiful human at a time – especially children – imagine the world we could create.

This is the next story I am writing for myself ...

I am rebuilding myself and how I show up in this world, one positive action at a time, and all my blocks *are* fitting back together, but differently.

I used to say when I was creating something – a show, a fundraiser, etc. – that 'I am too stupid to know when to stop', but all I was doing by saying that was making myself smaller, because I was too afraid to fully shine around others.

I've learnt that my light is a beacon for others and that, along with my voice – like yours – rises and shines to show others the way.

'I live this life now to honour my wife's time on this earth … and I wouldn't be doing that if I didn't do something powerful with mine.'

Tania Russell

45 | From: Auckland, Aotearoa, New Zealand | Lives: Auckland, Aotearoa, New Zealand

The next story I wish to see written for women is that we feel resourced, clear, calm and comfortable, flowing with life in ease and grace.

This is who I am in the world ...

I am a healer, and I now realise that we all are. To be alive is to experience the flow of health, of life moving through us – and this is what I understand healing to be.

Over the past fourteen years as a cranial osteopath, I have been fascinated to observe and facilitate this flow of health in the body and see it work its magic. More recently as a mind-body-heart practitioner, I've also seen how health can flow through restrictions in our mind, body or life, to calm, move through, enliven and restore.

This flow of health, the flow of life, feels to me like a river running through my hands. It can begin with a feeling of potential, light or spark and continues as a trickle, a feeling of warmth, a melting flow, spreading through the body. Easing through what's ready to be released, softening blocks and boulders along the way and bringing replenishment and renewal along its path. One of my favourite things is to observe this experience, and I wish everyone to know and feel it.

If we knew the healing potential of our bodies and how to tune into, feel and allow health to flow, we might not need to feel afraid of, block out or ignore what feels wrong.

I used to be more familiar with finding what was restricted, contracted or out of place in a body, and now others find this easier than me. While I experience this to be an essential part of healing, with love and compassion, what I see now is how finding what feels right, what feels like health, potential, light and spark, is what allows more of that to flow, which naturally harmonises and neutralises what is not.

I love assisting people to tune back into this health and feel it flow, be that in their body or in any aspect of their lives.

Realising that the power of feeling equals the power of healing, I am learning to love and appreciate sensitivity as the gift. I know I'm not alone in feeling sensitive. In the past, I wished I wasn't as it can feel bumpy, confusing, scary and overwhelming to feel things deeply.

I realise now that this sensitivity allows me to acutely feel in my body what feels right and wrong, what feels restricted or in ease, even before my mind can understand how or why. It also allows me to tune into my heart compass, my intuition, to feel, know and rediscover what feels true for me, soothing my way through.

I have loved discovering the power of the heart over the past five years through mind-body medicine, HeartMath and Golden Heart Wisdom. With the assistance of knowing how to tune into my heart to harmonise, neutralise, clarify and enhance, I find it increasingly easier to navigate life more smoothly and enjoyably. I absolutely love my role as a Golden Heart Wisdom ambassador as I excitedly explore and experience more of our heart's potential.

I am continually evolving and expanding, as a curious explorer of human potential, of possibility and what we don't know yet. At age eleven, the book *Mind Power* by John Kehoe piqued my interest, appreciating even then that maybe we don't know all there is to know about how the mind works. I've discovered similarly about the body and the heart along the way. The reality that there is always more possible is an exciting way to live!

These continued explorations through mind, body, heart and life, through yoga, meditation, dance, nature and healing, give me deep peace and hope for the future. For women, humanity and our relationships with each other and our world.

This is the next story I want written for women ...

The story I wish to see next written for women is where we feel and know more of our true selves and true potential.

Where we feel resourced, clear, calm and comfortable, flowing with life in ease and grace. That we know our sensitivity as a gift, comfortable in allowing sensations and healing to flow and harmonise through us. That we can live tuned into and navigating from our heart centres, expressing more of our true selves in the world.

This is ourself beneath limitations, judgements, quick reactions or frustrating repeating patterns. The true self we know when everything feels aligned and in sync. When we're fully present in the moment and there's nowhere else we'd rather be, naturally beautiful, kind and fun. The one who knows exactly what to do and when to do it, yet with all the time in the world. The one who navigates by intuition and acts with intelligence and compassion. The one who naturally honours herself and others, while being playful, enjoying and appreciating life. The one we knew better when we were a child, who is open to receive, love and share.

Beyond this, I'm fascinated to see what else is possible for women that we don't know yet!

This is the next story I am writing for myself ...

I wish to continue to live guided and harmonised by my heart. To know and express my unique essence. To feel free to be all of me.

I would like to let myself enjoy it a little more, to be playful and have more fun.

To feel comfortable and integrated with abundance and ease.

To let myself spend more time receiving and appreciating.

To be as generous to myself as I am to others.

To dance more, enjoy more time in nature, laugh more and connect more.

To move gracefully, easily and effortlessly through life.

To remember that as I allow all of this, I allow it for others too.

To let inspirations flow, see and enjoy them as they come to life. To expand, assist and enjoy one-to-one sessions, healing spaces, resources and experiences, online and in person, and feel comfortable receiving rewards for the rewards others experience in these too.

To see the benefits of health flow on and expand.

Yasmine Walker

52 | From: Port Moresby, Papua New Guinea | Lives: Canberra, Australia

All women deserve success, to be honoured for their individuality and for what they bring to the table and society.

This is who I am in the world …

I'm blessed to be mixed race with Italian, Papua New Guinean, German, Spanish/Filipino (mother's side) and Chinese-Malaysian (Father's side) heritage. My family history is fascinating, but this is for another time.

I'm often described by my friends and colleagues as being a calm, always smiley and happy being. I believe this to be true, and I have been since I was a child, even in the darkest of times.

When I look back on life there have been significant anchors, both light and dark, that have made me who I am in the world; there is nothing in my life that I regret or resent.

As a young person, I was a victim of physical and verbal abuse at school. At the age of five, I was singled out by a teacher, made to stand in front of the class and was beaten over mathematical fractions.

In family life, we experienced and witnessed domestic and family violence and abuse in all its forms – physical, sexual, emotional and mental.

In my teenage years, sexual abuse reared its head. Armed with wisdom from my younger years, I knew the signs and what to do. The thing that sticks most was not the abuse (odd, I know), but not being believed by those I placed my trust and love in to help my vulnerable and afraid self.

As a young adult and later a mother, the complexities, pressures of life and untreated childhood and teenage trauma saw me tumble deeply into a clinical depression to the point that I attempted suicide three times. My first attempt was when I was seventeen years old.

Fast-forward to the time between 2008 and the present.

Today, I'm proud to say that I am a successful intrapreneur and have surpassed my expectation of who I would become, even without a degree. Simply a strong work ethic and desire to rise to the top at what I did was what saw me move through my career very fast and achieve everything I desired.

So, what has been my special sauce, you ask. Well, you see, I have always believed that each of us is made for something very special. We are divine beings that are here to create the art of the possible – *our* possible.

I believe in the magic of things. That is, if we truly desire something and do the work, we can absolutely achieve it. For me, there are a handful of significant anchors in my life that helped me then and still to this day are an imprint of my life transcended.

My anchors:

Santa Claus. I remember seeing him one Christmas; he playfully hid behind boxes as my aunt called me upstairs to show me that Santa had brought me a doll for Christmas! At the time, my parents could never afford a doll like this.

Easter Bunny. Wanting so much to see what the Easter Bunny had left, with sadness seeing my friend next door get visited by the Easter Bunny made me wish for the same. As I wished with all my being, something whispered to me to look in the bushes, and there it was! One little aqua-blue-wrapped Easter egg for me to enjoy.

As an adult, my anchors were two books that really changed my perception, healed me and got me out of the deep dark holes of clinical depression.

My Story by Dave Pelzer and *The Courage to Heal* by Ellen Bass and Laura Davis. I used these books to propel my own healing. Inspired by the stories of others, it gave me the strength to heal myself and started me on a lifelong desire to help others to heal themselves too.

These memories are so significant and strong, and no-one can tell me that the Easter Bunny or Santa were a figment of my imagination. Maybe it wasn't Santa or the Easter Bunny, but an angel. No matter what you believe, the energy behind believing in something greater and our will to create beyond our current reality counts, and we have the power to transform, make our own 'art of the possible' and heal.

This is the next story I want written for women …

Through my work as an NLP coach, mentor and mindfulness and meditation teacher, I'd like to provide women with the tools, skills and strength to tap into their inner and outer resources and be at the forefront of change globally.

Let women stand in their power with all their being and in all arenas – in their families, society, work, politics and communities. All women deserve success, to be honoured for their individuality and for what they bring to the table and society.

I want men, sons and husbands to be proud of women, to support and love them, be emotional with them and celebrate them. In turn, women should reciprocate the same for the deserving men in their lives.

This is the next story I am writing for myself …

My story for the next five years and beyond is to be a successful entrepreneur in both corporate and private coaching, mentoring and healing so that I can enable individuals, the community and society to transform those who are willing and ready.

I will be a bestselling author, an inspiring and well sought-after thought leader to both young and old and will provide a path for them to pursue the art of the possible in their goals, purpose and vision.

I will stand in my power with compassion and strength as a mother, wife, leader and as a role model to others that anything is possible if you truly desire, believe and act.

Finally, as Peter Drucker said, 'The best way to predict the future is to create it.'

Penelope Prana

9.5 (life begins at 40, right!?) | From: Adelaide Hills, South Australia | Lives: Barossa Valley, South Australia

My wish for you. That you truly understand your ability to tap into the limitless power of your inner resources and have the confidence and language to compassionately articulate what's important to you and why.

Power, Purpose, Numb.
Dis-ease, distract. Who am I?
Yin Yang, Karuna.
My story is not one of trauma, catastrophe or hardship. I'm a privileged white woman, living in a First World country and have earned my living from behind a desk.

This is who I am in the world ...

I am lucky. I had a wonderful childhood playing with horses and as an adult had the opportunity to attend university. So why the confusion around who I am? Why the numbness, disease and distraction?

For the past decade I've lived between two realms: IT professional Monday to Friday and fire-spinning, hula-hooping yogacharini on weekends! Five years living off grid (one without electricity) highlighted this incongruity. Living simply, surrounded by mountains and rainforest, using an outdoor bathroom and camp kitchen opened my mind to different ways of being and helped realign my priorities.

As a child I recall receiving sage advice 'just be you'. Simple enough, or is it? I'm a people-pleaser. I quickly learnt to give people the responses they wanted. At school it was easier to give the answer being sought, rather than question the situation or challenge the vision. I was a model student, but there was no course on how to be ME.

As an adult, yogic philosophy guides my thoughts, words and actions. I strive to do no harm (ahimsa), act with compassion (karuna) and speak my truth (satya). I'm strong, determined and shy (although most people wouldn't recognise that last trait in me).

I've worked in spaces where people's words and actions are contradictory. Where politicking is the norm and marketing abounds. Where ego is aligned with success and the biggest bully comes out on top. Position power! Power clicks! Power grouping!

Playing roles I didn't resonate with chipped away at my happiness. I became hardened, conditioned to believe the traditional patriarchal approach is the only way to get results.

It's exhausting fighting your destiny.

For me, the consequence was losing the will to live, slowly – not spectacularly, but insidiously over time. Losing enthusiasm and curiosity for the world. No wonder I was grossly deviating from the plan the universe had in mind for me. When I listened, I realised my body and mind were screaming at me, begging me to change.

I've required some radical self-care to heal the scars of perpetually working under stress. I credit Nimbin University (the ten-year Nimbin lived experience) with deprogramming my early conditioning and redefining my purpose. The solution to my depressed state lay in the subtle practices of yoga and the playful influence of the hula hoop. Hooping helps me let go and find my flow, not just with the hoop, but in life too. Yoga taught me to connect and to sit in discomfort when necessary.

I became part of a few wonderful communities during my time in the Northern Rivers. I came to appreciate the healing potential of an alternative lifestyle, including drumming circles, fire spinning, poetry, art, music and holistic medicine.

After decades spent supporting stereotypical masculine rules, I now know there's a strength within the matriarchy, a supportive power where we grow stronger together and no-one is left behind unless they choose to be (inclusive of all gender roles).

This is the next story I want written for women ...

My wish for you is that you truly understand your ability to tap into the limitless power of your inner resources and have the confidence and language to compassionately articulate what's important to you and why. To dare to be vulnerable, in the knowledge that vulnerability and strength can coexist.

I wish for a rebalancing of Shiva and Shakti (the masculine and feminine energies). For too long, feminine energy has been repressed and the masculine permitted to grow beyond usefulness. I've seen good intentions and pure-hearted ambitions turn sour whilst women model their success on the ways of men, gradually adopting egocentric ways of being and unhealthy habits in communication.

I wish for you to have access to the life-changing resources that I embrace. To live in a time with a changed definition of success; where those who demonstrate kindness, compassion and cooperation are applauded, and choosing adrenal fatigue and a cold list of achievements is seen as foolish.

I'd like for you to embrace your feminine power and build a new paradigm, based on mutual purpose, cooperation, respect, openness and trust. Structures with less rigidity, individual empowerment and the ability to pivot instead of supporting outdated systems. I wish for a move away from egocentric and towards heart-centric leadership. Where leadership is earned and re-earned, not taken for granted.

This is the next story I am writing for myself ...

It is so tempting to focus on all the things I'm done with, the mistakes I've made that I'll not repeat, but without those learnings I would not be me and I would not have the wisdom I need to complete the next chapter, so in the spirit of santosa (acceptance of what is), I forgive myself for all the mistakes I've made and those that are yet to come.

I am yogacharini Penelope Prana. I nurture and listen to my intuition, for I know this is intelligence of a higher source. I'm interested in real conversations, real relationships and am accepting of the ebb and flow of the universe. I'm forever both teacher and student, for together we make magic.

I unapologetically bring my true self to each role I undertake. My work is unique because it comes from my creative space. The habits I create today are those I know will serve me well in the long-term.

I rise as an elder within my communities and openly share learned wisdom, helping others to be their best self by engaging in radical self-care and connected living. I heal myself with whole plant remedies and energy medicine. By giving people a glimpse of an alternative way of being that is in tune with our planet, I contribute to the wellbeing of others and the planet we live on.

Laura Morrice

42 | From: Scotland | Lives: Fraserburgh, Scotland

The world is our playground in which we can create anything and everything, and by choosing to align with love, hopefully, we can leave it better for future generations.

This is who I am in the world ...

Now I am a healer, wife, mother and author. Now I am more in tune with my divine nature than ever before. I am now fully connected with source through a greater sense of awareness which, in turn, is allowing me to be me, in my wholeness, unapologetically – but it wasn't always this way.

The affliction of addiction shaped much of my younger years; firstly, I witnessed my mum as she tried to soothe her traumas with alcohol and then later, with my own heroin addiction that changed the course of everything. Unbeknown to me at the time, this part of my life would then go on to help me heal my wounds and the generational conditioning that had been passed down.

But life had to take me to a much greater depth of despair before I was ready to undertake the healing that would ultimately set me free and enable me to live my truth with confidence and conviction.

I'd been in a relationship with my then-partner for around five years, and by this point, anger, despair and resentment were the dominating undertones. There I was, in my living room, and not a word was being spoken between us. As he sat there drinking beer and listening to music with headphones on, which had become the norm for weeks, my heart started to race and I felt a wave of sadness come over me as the truth of my situation hit me like a punch in the guts.

I didn't know who I was anymore. Through not following my gut instincts for so long, I had lost myself and become a shell of the person I used to be. Even I struggled to believe that I was once a person full of positivity, effervescence and zest for life. Instead, I felt like a failure – pathetic and weak – and this was hard for me to accept.

That was the moment I was ready to take responsibility for all of my choices, the good and the bad. It was what the universe had been waiting for, and it then catapulted me into the world of energy healing, which I soaked up like a long-forgotten truth.

After years of fine-tuning my gifts through practical experience and learning to join the dots of negative influences in my life, I now specialise in the removal and understanding of blockages, negative paradigms and limiting beliefs. Sharing this unique healing style and my journey with my clients helps them make sense of life's contrast instead of pushing against it constantly.

My healing journey continues to bring me into greater alignment with source energy. As a result, I can be even more authentic in providing loving inspiration to the collective. Which, in turn, becomes a guiding light for others seeking to reconnect with their truth at a soul level.

This is the next story I want written for women …

For too long, women have lived disconnected from their truth and divine purpose; we are the birthers and nurturers of creation! Programmed by so many contradictions that it's no wonder we have a hard time accepting it when the universe starts to throw breadcrumbs our way.

There is a power struggle between the masculine and feminine when there ought to be balance. Without balance, energy descends into more evident chaos, which is hard to ignore in today's world.

I want women to understand the importance of their unique alignment and seek out their individuality with confidence, courage and conviction. And then weave that into the limitless fabric of the universe for positive change and growth.

Taking responsibility for the good and the bad turns stories of victimhood into foundations of strength instead of weaknesses that we should feel ashamed of. Then women can rise with inner power, borne of an understanding of unconditional love, which will have a butterfly effect for now and future generations.

A woman's place in this world has become twisted beyond all recognition so that we willingly give up our sense of pride for our divine nature and falsely accept paths in life that have little or no room for living from our heart centres.

My greatest wish is that the collective consciousness rises to a new level of understanding and awareness, borne out of unconditional love for all life. And for women to grasp just how essential their role is in paving the way for this bright new future.

This is the next story I am writing for myself ...

My future account is one of quantum leaps in all areas of life and is a constant source of inspiration for others seeking to find that sense of wholeness and meaning. But do this in ways that bring more joy, love and happiness, three vital ingredients for life!

For my book *Signposts to Source* to become a *New York Times* bestseller (and more!) to help make spirituality not only more relatable but also undeniable for those not yet familiar with this aspect of their being; we are, after all, spiritual beings having a human experience.

I will continue to empower others to be their own magic wand by opening them up to the ancient knowledge of our energy systems (chakras) to understand their one-of-a-kind make-up. So that they, too, can reveal the inner light that the world so desperately needs right now and then bear witness to the beauty that unfolds.

The story that continues to unfold as I journey through life has my purpose attached to every word helping to raise humanity's collective consciousness. The world is our playground in which we can create anything and everything, and by choosing to align with love, hopefully, we can leave it better for future generations.

No matter what the future holds for me, I will continue to grow and evolve to be a better me, a better mum, a better wife – better in all ways for my own sense of satisfaction so that when my time of transition comes, I feel content with having given life my all while honouring the soul contract I came here to fulfil. Forever grateful!

Gaelyn Miriam Larrick

71 | From: Philadelphia, USA | Lives: Ubud, Bali

I hold a deep desire for women to be raised in an atmosphere of appreciation and support so that they embody who they truly are and shape the trajectory of humanity.

This is who I am in the world ...

Ever since I was a child, I have been making art. From painting to sculpting to acting, I created something out of nothing with anything I could get my hands on. Originally from Philadelphia, USA, my life has been – in its own way – a work of art. When I started out my creative career as a model, I had no idea where it would take me. I soon discovered that being paid to be a 'human hanger' for clothing and having unreasonable weight requirements foisted on me was not how I wanted to live my life.

Fast-forward fifty years and I am content and settled in an amazingly eclectic community in Bali, at the heart of it all in Ubud. My art these days is easily inspired by beauty everywhere. My intention is to bring out the magnificence in the layers of every landscape and image with which I work. I have discovered that cultivating an appreciation of what is already around and within me allows me to access the natural radiance in everything.

My primary intention is to create inner peace through art. When I look back to the years when I was an activist during the Vietnam war, I can see now that fighting against something takes the focus from creating what you want from within. Peace and beauty go hand in hand.

I feel my work comes *through* me, not *to* me. I have learned, over many years of creating art, that I am able to create a request even if I'm not familiar with what I'm creating. For me, art is where I step into a mode of free form in which even I don't know where it will go.

When I begin an art project, all my creative skills come together to reflect an aspect of each woman's healing and depth. I believe we are all so much deeper than what the surface portrays, and I create images that embody the spirit of each subject. My art has been a product of my own healing journey, and every stage and nuance has led me to a different way of expressing divinity. My intention when I work with any subject is to bring out the archetypal energy that is asking for fuller expression in the life of every woman, to honour and celebrate where she is on her path. I often feel the process of art itself is a desire to both create beauty in the world and heal what needs to be seen and loved. Art offers us a way to see our own beauty, and my passion lies in helping each woman see the abundant magnificence of who they truly are.

This is the next story I want written for women ...

I hold a deep desire for women to be raised in an atmosphere of appreciation and support so that it is a natural consequence that women embody who they truly are and shape the trajectory of humanity in powerful ways. I believe we are all on a healing journey, one that requires claiming one's own power and ability to do anything our heart desires. The power of sisterhood and recognition must allow each woman to feel free to express exactly who she is. Regardless of social conditioning, where she is from, or the burdens she carries, I aim to reflect each woman's true strength and essence in my art. My vision is a world where women are surrounded by people who encourage them to follow their excitement and truth, knowing that anything and everything is possible.

I see a world coming where the value of the divine feminine is finally honoured and respected; a world where every woman knows her own power without competing or dimming her own light. Far beyond the constructs of accepted capabilities, I support women embracing their own beauty, purpose and passion, wherever that takes them. I believe I am an early start to the inevitable claim that women will one day rise to meet their own beauty and worth. My role is to simply reflect this shift as I create images that capture the soul essence and message of every woman.

This is the next story I am writing for myself ...

My next focus is creating a home that both nurtures and allows me the space and time to relax deeper and create more. I envision a gorgeous tropical nature view and enough space for my friends and community to gather and visit. Though I continue to enjoy and explore Bali, I feel this next stage of life is about turning within and creating something that I have yet to create and experience myself.

I am very grateful to be doing the work that speaks the most to my heart and that I came here to do. I create pieces I call 'magical power talismans' – scenes and images that bring in ancient symbolism and designs that embody the spirit of each woman. I create the piece to reflect the process that particular woman is on, her mission here on earth and where she is at currently. It can serve her as a 'focusing device' – similar to a vision board – that encourages her every day to embody the person and energy she sees in the picture.

I have an amazing business partner who has helped me co-host successful workshops for women and our next vision is to bring in the wisdom that our last decade taught us (while we were each creating individually on different continents) together. We intend to host our work internationally, beginning in Africa. We want our reach to be limitless.

My next chapter is based on sharing my perspective of how this universe is set up and tools and practices that can help people navigate it. I share this to uplift others and give them a wider view with which to appreciate life beyond their day-to-day reality.

I will continue to explore new art mediums and techniques to expand and explore what is possible through my photography and art. I invoke simply the ideal location to do so and the space to bring forth a lifetime of creativity and passionate living.

Sharon Chemello

60 | From: Malaysia | Lives: Brisbane, Australia

Heal yourself to help your daughter, partner, son, family, friends, pets, workmates. Change your DNA, heal ancestral trauma. Start your journey, help is everywhere.

This is who I am in the world ...

I'm known as Aunty Shazza, S-Dawg, Shazza, 'The Families and Teens Whisperer', Mermaid.

For my sixtieth, I want a balloon ride, a party at the beach or home. Live to ninety. At fifty-three my own life really started.

Brisbane since fifteen, from Malaysia. A beautiful affinity with Indonesia and its people. Dad was in the Air Force, so we moved around Australia. Moved to the north side of Brisbane to live with Frank at Brighton, and the beach is my haven. I have a crazy little dog, and I'm a stepmum and step-grandma.

A healing journey – from rock bottom to thriving. I've rebuilt a life writing books, coaching, teaching and living with love. A current journey with melanoma is bringing me back to the importance of living life to the fullest. I'm ready to work through it and remind people to get out of their heads, into their hearts, focus on love, mission, purpose, build a happy, worry-free life.

A challenging upbringing, not so warm and fuzzy, but love shown in other ways. Mum managed everything. They did their best, but all family members were troubled. Dad left us after Malaysia – ran off with a younger woman. I became a teacher which Mum wanted. Married at twenty-three into an Italian family. Left teaching, worked in sales and marketing for educational publishers. I had my two beautiful kids with IVF. A helicopter mum. The ex was ladder-climbing and building our property portfolio.

Lost many family members to cancer and a baby. Grief is a big part of what happened. I was a mostly stay-at-home mum and relief teacher. I needed to find and create myself, always looking for answers, needing a mission or purpose. Took on people's problems and projects to avoid my own pain. A time bomb.

My kids – Marco, twenty-five, married, and Lisa, twenty-three, partnered – are my joy and deepest connection along with my partner, friends, family, pets and nature. Postnatal depression affected me badly. Anxiety and depression were part of my life for a long time. Limiting beliefs, guilt, shame and feelings of unworthiness. Drinking heavily towards the end of the marriage, I was a self-sabotaging mess. Other things happened in the relationship which led to me finding a connection outside my marriage.

Separated, then divorced, I hit rock bottom again. Depression and anxiety, long days, lonely nights. Drinking, bad dating, bad TV and medication. Crying. A slow road to recovery using books, courses, coaching, alternate therapies. My kids and mates kept me going. Coaching, personal development studies, changes I made, including sobriety. A bucket list of surfing, dancing, skateboarding, skydiving.

A leader and influencer. Frank and I teach sustainable living in our group Sustainable Crusaders, incorporating waste, lifestyle, relationships, mental health. I run Facebook groups for confidence, families, coaching and a group for my book *EMOJI: Find your Happy Face,* which is out later this year. EMOJI is an acronym for wellness strategies I have found useful to reduce anxiety and depression and find peace, calm, surrender, acceptance, stillness and joy! Energy, emotions, EFT (tapping), exercise, mindfulness, meditation and so on. Vital parts are the ownership of our problems and the inner healing, inner child.

I am living proof that you can transform your life. Do I have regrets? Hell yeah. Would I wish I could have done it differently? You bet. But we only know what we know, doing the best we can at the time with what we have. The secret is to listen, learn and become aware, so we raise our vibration, be well and pay it forward.

This is the next story I want written for women ...

Heal yourself to help your daughter, partner, son, family, friends, pets, workmates.

Change your DNA, heal ancestral trauma. Start your journey, help is everywhere.

I want women to know they can do anything, from the women on construction sites in Malaysia, to my friend, a short, feminine blonde, CEO of a major textile business in Melbourne, to my bridesmaid's daughter, a top apprentice mechanic.

I wanted to be a psychologist, but my mum encouraged me to be a teacher. I found a way to study psychology through teaching and coaching, and my message is that you can do whatever you want and fulfil your dreams.

Sing, dance, eat, pray, love, travel – all the things. Start your bucket list. Heal relationships. Get into meditation, the pilgrimage, yoga camp, life-changing stuff! Support others. Teach mean girls. Make sure you're not one, nor your daughter or friends. Lift others and champion them. Live your life to the full in a gentle caring way. Show you and your inner child love and kindness.

This is the next story I am writing for myself …

I recently had a cancer scare: a lump on my knee led to a whirlwind of tests and medical appointments. Melanoma. Next step is immunotherapy. Finding out was hard, reactions then responses. Anger that I've just been through a roller-coaster and deserve a break. There were tears of grief and fear. Then came the response: *How do I heal this?* Alternatives, exercise, meditation, nutrition. A trip to Bali to see Ketut Liyar, the healing man who I saw four years ago. Mexico where alternate doctors are working. I told my beautiful daughter, as she wept, that if I must climb the Tibetan mountains to drink the nectar from the rare lily, I'm there!

I encourage everyone to live life to the fullest. Create and thrive, rather than survive. I watch people at the hospital who should be enjoying their years; instead, they are having treatment for illnesses, many preventable. 'What are you all doing here? You should be off travelling, playing with grandchildren, children, pets.'

My partner and I will take a caravan lap of Australia as the Sustainable Crusaders. Take my adult kids somewhere special; see friends in Canada and Uluru. My *EMOJI* book, accompanying program, maybe an app. Currently teaching arts at a little school at Woody Point, relief teaching at other schools. On a break for my knee operation.

Writing, paperwork, spring cleaning, catching my breath and implementing *EMOJI* strategies. I'd never have dealt with this well a few years back. Things happen at the right time, coming to teach us. Listening and learning, I've rewritten my story. I'll heal the big C, my courageous journey. If I can't, I'll face that with dignity and courage. But I have a good feeling. I'm not done yet!

Much love to all, Aunty Shazza, Sharon Chemello.

Charlott Kisvarda

49 | From: Stockholm, Sweden | Lives: Mount Dandenong Ranges, Melbourne, Australia

It is a privilege to be living this human experience as a woman, and yet I feel deeply compassionate for women near and far who for various reasons are unable to experience life in equality.

'Loving who you are and embracing all that you can be and do is the ultimate privilege in being human.' – Charlott Kisvarda

This is who I am in the world ...

I am an intuitive mindset coach and have expanded in my services as a psychic medium. Embracing my intuition has been a pivotal point in my own evolution.

I was born in Sweden, and I now reside in the beautiful temperate forest of the Dandenong Ranges in Australia with my family.

During childhood I recall having a connection to the spirit world, sensing and communicating with the unseen. My dreams were profound, and I sensed things before they happened. It wasn't something I openly discussed with others; it was just how I navigated through the world. I didn't equate it back then to being psychic, I considered it to be my wild, yet accurate, imagination and it served me well in predicting outcomes and guiding me through decisions and directions in my life.

My twenties and thirties were filled with study, travel, work and setting up home with my husband and young children. I switched careers from fashion illustration to pursuing my passion in personal development, studying human behaviour. I wanted to explore a career where I could be of service to others. During my training in life coaching, we were encouraged to dump 'magical thinking' and that 'signs' are nonsense. From this, I struggled with my spiritual beliefs, and this is where the conflict between science and spirituality came about for me. I can now appreciate the balance between the two and how it works in harmony.

When I settled in Mount Dandenong, my forest home, connected with nature and felt aligned in my life, I opened up this magical world of connecting to spirit again.

I've always been a highly visual person – I would consider myself to be clairvoyant, seeing moving images in my mind's eye, as if a movie is playing out in front of me. Several years ago, I attended a sound meditation, and what I experienced took me to another level I had never experienced before. Feeling into a deep state of relaxation, the visuals in my mind began to swirl. Deeper in, I experienced a profound shift in all my senses. I had a profound awakening to my gifts opening again.

Several days later, I noticed changes within me, all my senses were heightened. This could be considered an improvement, but I was unravelling. Nothing was as if it was before, and this confused me. I heard thoughts that didn't appear to be my own. I could smell cigarette smoke or perfume when there was no evidence that someone close by was smoking or wearing perfume. I was seeing flashes of sparkling lights and figured shadows with the sense of someone in the room. I honestly thought I was losing my mind.

Over time, I grew more comfortable with who I was becoming, or rather, who I always was, yet had disconnected from. The more I opened my expansion on sensing, the more I sought to give intuitive guidance to others.

Now my passion and purpose is being in service to others. Combining my learnings in intuitive coaching and mindset strategies, I empower people to tap into their own intuition and guide them back to their authentic self. I also love to connect people with their loved ones who have passed. I believe our human experience is greatly made up of the connection and relationship we have with ourselves and with others. Being able to support people through their personal connections gives me immense satisfaction.

This is the next story I want written for women ...

Our connection to self and each other can be our greatest achievement in life. As a woman, I feel deeply connected to the miracle of life, creating and birthing human life into this world. Guiding my children is my deepest joy. I feel it is a privilege to be living this human experience as a woman, and yet I feel deeply compassionate for other women near and far who, for various reasons, are unable to experience life in equality. Ever since I was a child, I believed the world was our playground to explore and learn from. I want all women to have the opportunity to experience life abundantly. I adore sisterhood and the connection women have with each other. More women in leadership and of influence would be an honour to witness in this lifetime. I strive to encourage and empower all the women who choose to work with me to be living extraordinary lives, gifting the world with their magic.

This is the next story I am writing for myself ...

Coming close to half a century of living life here on earth and an intent to live the next fifty years abundantly, I reflect with gratitude for all that I have experienced thus far. There have been challenges that have shaped me, and those moments are some of my greatest gifts in wisdom. Mostly, life has been beautifully graced with amazing people who share this time and space with me. As I continue to learn, grow and evolve, I choose to see the best in people, knowing we are all here to learn, love and live as best we can. Each of us has a path as individual as we are. Every day is a gift to explore more about ourselves and others, to connect more, give more and be more. My next chapter in life I will continue to be in service, supporting others to shine. There are so many opportunities to give back to our community and our planet. I want to contribute by supporting others in their endeavours to improve our world for the better.

Erin Pintar

55 | From: Melbourne, Australia | Lives: Melbourne, Australia

I want women to understand that they do not have to fit a criteria to be beautiful, and that at the very essence of their souls, they are beauty.

This is who I am in the world …

I am a mother of four, an adventurous individual and loyal friend. Compassionate and caring, I am a fighter for myself and for many, advocating for those who need support and guidance.

I am a beach lover, a dreamer with a massive curiosity for human behaviour. I am a student of life, forever growing and learning.

My titles include founder of Soul Purpose Consulting, master coach, NLP practitioner, hypnotherapist, trainer, behavioural profiler and author.

I am a grandparent, honouring this role by being as 'GRAND' as I can be, in the love I give, the life wisdom I share, through the resilience I foster to help him to develop and the space I create to grow into his beautiful and unique self.

Growing up in a large family with alcohol-fuelled abuse, I became a timid, insecure young lady without a voice of my own. Not only did I become a people-pleaser, fearing that I wouldn't be liked if I didn't do what was asked of me, I never stood up or spoke for myself, leaving my confidence at rock bottom.

During my marriage, on one particular day, my husband, very disgruntled, expressed himself rudely and abruptly in our lounge room, before storming outside. We were left on the familiar eggshells that we often walked upon. Turning to my teenage children, I reminded them that they do not have to put up with that! Looking at me, they agreed, but also appeared confused. In that moment, I realised that what I said and what I did were misaligned, as I was in fact tolerating this exact behaviour. I knew that things had to change.

My youngest child is deaf and has a cochlear implant to assist his hearing. One day, my son, around twelve years old, and I left an appointment at the hospital where they would expand all facets and volume of his processor to try and broaden his hearing range by computer. Driving home, he asked me if he was speaking loudly. I assured him that he wasn't and asked him why. He replied, 'I CAN HEAR MY VOICE.'

With surprise, I thought, *Oh my God!* I had never realised my son hadn't heard himself speak previously. Through tears of joy, we celebrated all the way home, stopping to hear the birds sing. As he grew up, I had been a voice for my son, and through this, I had found my own. These two events became the catalyst for me ending my thirty-year relationship. Unsure of what the future held, I trusted that I knew we were going to be just fine.

Everyone has a story, and they vary to mine, and yet I meet so many people that are stuck! Stuck in a job, relationship, stuck in a role they feel they have to play in life, and many don't know how to get out and move forward. I am here to tell you that it is possible.

I have met so many inspiring women that I am forever in awe of who have overcome and excelled after horrific childhoods and past events. It reminds me constantly of the strength, capability and resilience that females possess, and that it is entirely possible to unlock these tools.

This is the next story I want written for women ...

I want the next story for women to be one of opportunity and love. To know we're not just daughters, sisters, wives or mothers. And we are certainly not the labels that society or social media may give us, that we are too old, too fat, too thin, unattractive or not good enough.

I want women to understand that they do not have to fit a criteria to be beautiful, and that at the very essence of their souls they are beauty. Beauty that doesn't come from fashion, their skin colour or body shape. I want all women to know their worth, to accept themselves in their glory and in how much value they bring to everybody.

I want education and information available to parents and young women to ensure they grow up in safe environments. To learn not to give away their power by measuring themselves based on the opinions of others, society and the validation of their social media friends.

I want women to embrace and support other women instead of judging and criticising based on perceived 'enoughness'. I want women to get out of their heads and into their hearts, coming from a place of love.

I want women to know that their self-worth comes from within, having the courage to challenge their fears and leave situations, relationships, friendships and old beliefs that don't serve them anymore. It's time for all of us, young and old, to stand up and have a voice without fear or judgement.

We can create infinite possibilities for women's future and extend ripple effects to others through those who have experienced the role modelling of other women and been brave enough to also do this for themselves.

This is the next story I am writing for myself ...

I will continue my vision and mission through retreats, programs and workshops. I am grateful to have had the experiences on my journey thus far, including the mistakes, lessons, laughter and tears.

I am so proud of the programs I have designed that support women to excel in their confidence, have certainty in themselves and manage themselves in all situations. Witnessing a woman who feels stuck, with low self-belief or hidden purpose, blossom into a confident, resilient woman who freely expresses herself and speaks her truth, while also being her unique self, is the most beautiful and fulfilling job I have had.

I plan to embrace my adventurous side more, travelling to many destinations and making amazing connections with incredible people, hearing their stories and learning about their life journeys.

My future looks bright and colourful with new learnings, experiences and locations, allowing me to pass on my wisdom and life experience to everybody who needs it. My work in this lifetime is forever evolving, as am I.

Jinju Dasalla

45 | From: USA | Lives: Ubud, Bali, Indonesia

Who knew it could be so simple? That so much can be healed with a little bit of movement and a lot of love and compassion.

This is who I am in the world ...

Aloha, I'm Jinju.

I am a sacred weaver.

Who I am is who we all are – I am a humble, mysterious, expression of the divine.

I dance the sacred patterns of the cosmos, the cycles of nature, and embrace the spiral paths that guide us back home to the wisdom within. I weave the universal threads of science, soul and soma in service to divine feminine awakening within and all around.

My birth name is Pearl. I go by Jinju to embrace my Korean roots and because Jinju means 'authentic pearl' in Chinese. I am a doctor of neuroscience, a passionate educator, an eternal student of life, the creator of the healing modality, NeuroSomatic Flow, NaiAsana Yoga, and author of upcoming books, *The Goddess Brain* and *Awakening Fire with the Medicine of Flow*. I am a mentor and coach for women.

I am the proud forty-five-year-old mother of the most magical seven-year-old boy, Sekai Lokahi, and the proud wife of the most supportive, caring and loving man and father, Nova Dasalla. I am the daughter and only child of Chon Yong Cha and Robert Schroy.

Raised in a cross-cultural family, as a first-generation Asian-American, I am literally the bridge between worlds – east and west, yin and yang, science and spirituality, and beyond. It took me a couple of decades and much heartache to truly embrace the bridge that I am. As a child and teenager, I wanted more than anything to feel like I belonged to one world or the other.

Being ethnically mixed has come with many challenges, but I eventually came to see the bigger picture and deeper purpose – as a bridge between worlds.

I experienced a major turning point in 2004 when I left the modern biomedical world after deep frustration with modern medicine being so stuck in an imbalanced, non-holistic, outdated, patriarchal paradigm, that does not prioritise true healing.

Feeling lost, my plea for help was answered with an initiation into ancient wisdom teachings and an opportunity to spend time with indigenous medicine men and women deep in the Amazonian rainforests of Peru. This resulted in being shown my new path and excitement to serve my global family in a more inspired way.

My next major turning point was my own healing journey. Indeed, it was the bridging of two seemingly separate worlds, healing the split between my mind and my body, that held the key to my healing. While Western doctors insisted I suffered from a neurochemical imbalance, the real cause of my dis-ease was disconnection from my body, heart and soul, after years of being stuck in my head. Coming home to the sensual, somatic wisdom of my body has been one of the most enlightening journeys of my life.

The gateway to this healing journey was yoga and learning how to dance with poi, the hoop and fire. The poi and the fire, in particular, transformed my life and rewired my brain in such profound ways, this 'medicine of flow' became the foundation of the next chapter of my life's purpose and career.

Then, in 2015, I experienced an equally, if not more, profound awakening. Becoming pregnant and birthing a child into this world had me understand for the first time the underestimated and underappreciated wisdom and power of the womb and of the female brain.

Out of this birthed a new bridge, a clear calling – to support the rise of feminine consciousness, wisdom and leadership.

Today, I help women reactivate their 'goddess brains,' to know the biological and evolutionary basis of their divinity, beauty, wisdom and beyond.

I currently am living happily in Bali, Indonesia, with my husband and our seven-year-old son, where we run NaiAsa Institute, an international institute for somatic education, coaching and healing arts. We are also building a retreat sanctuary, divine feminine flow temple and tending our non-profit, Saraswati Seva Project, to help empower the women and families of Bali and beyond.

This is the next story I want written for women ...

Women have woken up to the truth of who they are, where they came from and their role in the evolution of consciousness.

Thanks to women rising up all around the world, today, in the year 2033, we celebrate the mass crumbling of patriarchy and the birth of a new Earth!

Since women became the new leaders of the world:

- There is no more war.
- Women are FREE to live, wander and express their full beauty without any concern for their safety or reputation.
- Sexual assault, rape and abuse are a thing of the past.
- We have clean air, water and soil.
- There is no more hunger.
- Neuroscientists announced the most exciting discoveries about the female brain and the womb leading to the new celebrated truth that women are biologically and neurophysiologically wired for so much more than most realised. Indeed, they are wired to LEAD!
- History has been rewritten to include *her*story.
- Health and happiness are not just for some humans, it's for all humans.

This is the next story I am writing for myself ...

Fast-forward to the ripe age of ninety. Reflecting back on the second half of my life, my entire being is filled with the most luminous sense of peace and fulfilment, knowing that our future generations will inherit the most beautiful, loving and abundant world possible.

Millions of women and their families were able to transform their lives and the lives around them, with the support of NaiAsa Institute and The Saraswati Seva Project.

My book, *The Goddess Brain,* became internationally acclaimed, translated into twenty-two languages and became a staple of the new education systems, assisting millions in embracing a whole new understanding of feminine consciousness, female neurophysiology and the powerful connections to the cosmos.

Millions more were able to benefit from the medicine of NeuroSomatic Flow™, especially as a way to not only release past trauma and constricting beliefs, but also to upgrade their nervous systems so they could keep up with the accelerated expansion of consciousness.

I am grateful I, along with my incredible family and dream team, was able to play a small but significant part in the awakening that got us here.

Om Santi Santi Santi Om.

Vicki Lark

63 | From: Adelaide, Australia | Lives: Melbourne, Australia

We are not born strong but we are forged in the fires we have had to walk through. We are the wild ones that will never be tamed. We are strong, powerful, resourceful, confident humans who will claw our way out of the pits of hell to arrive where we belong.

This is who I am in the world ...

I could say I am a mother, wife, widow, daughter, friend and colleague. But does that really explain who I am? It is only recently that I am starting to understand my true passion, my true identity. I am a puzzle, made up of many pieces that only recently have clicked together.

My mother fell pregnant out of wedlock in the 1950s and such was the time I was put up for adoption, and while I was told at eighteen, I did not learn her identity until I was in my fifties. While I have her name, I do not believe she is alive. My adopted parents died in separate car accidents six years apart when I was in my late teens. I felt so alone without any carers in the world. There were times when I contemplated my existence in this world but there was always a little voice at the back of my mind telling me my purpose was not yet discovered.

I joined the Army Reserves where I learnt teamwork, everybody working for a common goal. The Army was also where I met my husband, and we shared thirty-two years together. Some say that marriage is two kindred souls coming together in love; however, my experience was often of conflict, fear and grief. Unbeknownst to me, my husband struggled with alcohol addiction before we married, and over the years, addiction became the sole focus of our relationship and I became his carer. I grieved for the man I fell in love with, as he only appeared in moments of none or limited alcohol consumption. This period in my life taught me compassion, acceptance and the ability to identify the light through dark moments. My husband died in 2014 after battling tongue and neck cancer for nine months. I found myself alone with my two adult daughters still living at home. This left me pondering the meaning of life as I wasn't sure what lay beyond death, grief and lonesomeness.

While my daughters were growing up, I began volunteering with Girl Guides Victoria and Scouts Victoria to support my daughters' interests and it has turned into something I do for myself, as it brings me joy and satisfaction to provide opportunities for youth to develop confidence, resilience and a sense of belonging. I have held roles as a district manager and unit leader, and also worked with Melbourne Gang Show, a musical theatre production company, for the last twenty years. I believe children are our future and we need to invest in their youth and support their development, encouraging them to gain confidence in their abilities so they have success in our world.

My fifties were really a turning point as not only did I learn about my birth mother and my husband passed away, I also started my healing journey. I completed reiki level five training as well as exploring sound, colour, crystals and oils to complement this. I have also trained in angelic reiki, emotional clearing, dowsing, oils, flower essences and emotional freedom techniques (EFT). I am now an angelic reiki master teacher and healer and a member of the Angelic Reiki Association and the British Complementary Medicine Association (RMCA). I am most passionate about healing the physical, emotional, mental and spiritual bodies of my family, clients and the Earth through natural means.

This is the next story I want written for women ...

Women, how amazing are women?! I have noticed that women can break down temporarily, however, we always pick up the pieces, rebuild ourselves and come back stronger than before. We are not born strong, but we are forged in the fires we have had to walk through. We are the wild ones that will never be tamed. We are strong, powerful, resourceful, confident humans who will claw our way out of the pits of hell to arrive at where we belong.

Women are intricate beings that have so many abilities and talents. Look how we can juggle running a home, being social secretary to our partners and children, all while raising our children and going to work. We are the ultimate multitaskers. It is time for the world to view women as their own entities, rather than a commodity of another. It is time for women to step into their own light and have faith and confidence in themselves. Women have the capacity to do anything. It's a cliché that anything a man can do a woman can do too, but it is true. And if I'm not being too biased, they can do it just as well, if not better.

My wish for women is that they are empowered to take their health and happiness back into their own hands and find within themselves the tools to support the lives they deserve to live.

This is the next story I am writing for myself ...

I run a business where I empower women through showing them how to clear blockages and reclaim their strength and independence. I show them that any illness can be traced back to past and current emotions and that they can develop the skills to change their lives.

With the deaths of my adopted parents and my husband and discovering that I had been given up at birth, I have worked through abandonment issues, and this has motivated me to guide women to realise that our past is history and gives us wisdom, but it does not define us. Our future is a mystery. Our present is a gift that we can change. I explain to women that it is safe for us to take charge of our own life. We choose to be free, one step at a time.

Women often carry the weight of the world on their shoulders, but always manage to continue smiling through it all. This shows courage, bravery and resilience. I will continue to smile through the ups and downs, through the successes and challenges. Not because I want to disguise the pain, but because I choose happiness and gratitude for my path forward. This next chapter in my life is going to be the greatest yet.

Viviana Premazzi

41 | From: Venegono Inferiore, Varese, Italy | Lives: Sliema, Malta

I dream of a world where there is no more violence against women, where a culture of respect for differences and dignity for all prevails.

This is who I am in the world ...

My name is Viviana, and I am a global mindset developer, social entrepreneur, trainer, researcher and community worker.

What does this mean, 'global mindset developer'? It means my purpose is to help people develop an open and curious mindset about the world around them, promoting healthy, inclusive communities where everyone feels they can be their true selves and feel that they belong.

I am in my forties now and I strongly believe that everything happens for a reason, that my life has been shaped by the people I meet, and as Carl Jung would say, 'by meaningful coincidences'.

I come from a very closed community in Northern Italy. One of those places where everything is fine if you are part of the community and don't break any rules. You are included only if you agree and conform with 'the norm'. Everything coming from outside our cultural and religious community was always seen as problematic, a threat to our identity and sense of belonging. Along the years, I have seen this fear in many other communities around the world. Migration, my field of work and study, is a huge trigger for it. Migration brings diversity and change in communities, and it can easily become the scapegoat on many internal problems.

When I arrived in Malta in 2017, I had this strong desire to help the island and the communities there not to fear diversity, profoundly believing that with the right awareness, knowledge and skills, people would learn how to embrace and enjoy diversity in creating inclusive communities. Global Mindset Development, my company, is my baby and my dream; it's the dream of another possible world, of open communities, a world of peace, justice, opportunities and safety for all, a world with no oppression, no racism and discrimination.

This is the next story I want written for women …

It is comfortable to stay with people that we perceive as similar to us but there are individuals who have that constant feeling of restlessness, a strong desire to see what is outside … So as soon as I had the opportunity, and thanks to the support of my parents, I started travelling, studying and living in different countries. Portugal, Brazil, the USA and Malta, among others.

Every trip had an impact on my personal and professional life, but Brazil changed my life.

Among many beautiful things that happened to me in Brazil, I was also robbed for the first time in my life. I felt vulnerable. I felt unsafe. I felt the need for safety around me as an individual and especially as a woman. It is not the same travelling alone if you are a woman, and we, as women, know this. Despite this, I didn't let the fear stop me from discovering new places and I travelled alone to many countries.

The problem is that the fear was always with me, day and night, in cities or in the countryside. There are very few places where I felt safe being a woman and alone. In January 2022, a terrible episode of violence against a woman happened in Malta and it reminded me that as a society, we still have a long way to go and we need to keep working to destroy the toxic masculine culture – a culture where women are not safe, where it is easy to blame women for violence against women, where women should have their place in society next to a man, where men pretend to have rights and a say over women's bodies.

What I would like next written for women is the possibility to live in safety, to travel safely, to be what we want to be, to not need a man to give meaning to our life, to be able to dispose of our body, our mind and our choices. I dream of a world where there is no more violence against women, where a culture of respect for the differences and dignity for all prevails.

In loving memory of Paulina Dembska, Malta, 2 January 2022.

This is the next story I am writing for myself ...

In Brazil, I did the research for my dissertation. It was about *The Feminist Theology of Liberation for a Church and a Society Without Exclusion.* That, for me, was the starting point of a deep reflection about being a woman. I was raised to believe that a woman can only be a mother or a nun ... I felt I had no choice and no dignity in being just myself and without a man (being a human or Jesus Christ) ... It was extremely difficult to find my own identity and my place in the world ... *Who am I? Who do I want to be? Who* can *I be?*

And so here I am ... twenty years later: I am not a mother and I am not a nun, but I am a woman who was able to transform her passion into her profession, helping people not live in fear, embracing diversity and the world out there, being curious and open, planting seeds for change. I turned forty last year, and I am not a mother biologically. Still, I feel the social pressure every day with people asking, 'What's wrong with her?' 'Does she think her career is more important?' 'She is missing out ...' 'She will die alone ...'

I don't know if I will ever be a biological mother, but through my work I really feel, every day, I am a mother to many around me. My job is to listen, understand, nurture and accompany, as I see biological mothers do, to mentor my trainees in important choices in their life and to support young people who seek their voice and their role away from adults. In my work I feel I give birth every day, I create strong relationships – sometimes stronger than biological relationships. I support people to be themselves, different and unique, despite any external pressures. I want to be like this, I want to be myself, different and unique and to love who I am and the people around me despite our differences.

To my amazing partner, Roberto, who loves me for who I am.

Christina Fletcher

46 | Lives: Central Coast, NSW, Australia

I envision a community where women's intuitive and creative gifts and life-skills merge together to create something magical and for self-sustaining community living.

This is who I am in the world ...

To be honest, deep down I feel a little bit crazy, but in a cool-spiritual-chick kind of way. Since my spiritual awakening in 2007, I have been on one crazy journey. It wasn't easy at first, as I experienced my own 'dark night of the soul' where I had to dive deep into my own darkness and despair. I had to confront my entire life experience that was full of trauma, drama and instability.

This was a major turning point in my life. I didn't know any other so-called spiritual people, so I went on a journey to seek them out. I attended spiritual groups and festivals, hung out for hours talking to business owners in spiritual shops, experienced many weird and wonderful healing modalities and became addicted to intuitive card readings. I was experiencing a spiritual high, and my intuition was on point. These feelings of elation were new to me, because I was used to feeling anxious and depressed.

I completed my reiki master level in record time, and my teacher couldn't stop me on my mission. Random strangers would talk to me in public places, telling me stories of their loved ones that had passed away and I would channel the answers they were seeking and give them comfort. I felt like crows were stalking me, they seemed to be everywhere, cawing at me and they would come very close. It's no wonder I thought I was going crazy. I honestly thought that I could be experiencing a mental health crisis, as I felt ungrounded and found it difficult to process and integrate the conscious shifts that were taking place within me.

There was no model in the mainstream therapeutic arena that could hold a space of support for what I was experiencing. Although, I thought that labelling my experience as a mental illness would at least give me a break from all the craziness and perhaps there was a pill that could switch it all off. I realised that I wasn't going crazy after all, and it was only a spiritual awakening. Why me? And why did this happen?

As a child, I felt like I did not fit into this world; it was as if I knew that I was a visitor from another planet. I tried to fit in, with family, friends, external relationships, with the social norms, although this pathway never felt right for me. I felt alone and fearful and sensitive to everything in the environment surrounding me. I felt that something was still missing in my life. That something or someone was 'myself'. I had been living a temporary but false reality, an illusion that kept me thinking I was safe and also hidden in the world.

I was able to emerge from the depths of my despair and truly step into my own personal power. My life now is about connection within myself, to my spiritual source and to my soul friends and family. I accept and love myself authentically for who I am and not for what I think others should perceive me to be. I openly embrace my spiritual gifts and creativity. I have learnt to overcome mental, physical and emotional pain through my own self-healing practices and conscious awareness. I would describe myself as strong and also vulnerable. I am a warrior woman and also a gentle angel. I am a healer, an empath and nurturer.

My head is connected to heaven and my feet connected to the earth. I find serenity and the sense of feeling grounded in the healing elements of nature. I am loud and I have a voice that can roar like a tiger, and I am also silent and can connect quietly with my inner voice and soul. I am a quiet loner in a group of people, and I am also a leader and conscious space holder for others. Through my spiritual awakening journey, I now know what love, peace and freedom really is. I know that my true purpose in this lifetime is the role of a lightworker.

This is the next story I want written for women ...

I support women to have their own inner and outer voice and to feel empowered and connected within themselves and with their spiritual connection to source. I envision a world where women join together to support each other and lift each other's spirits. I encourage women to harness their intuition and creative gifts and life skills, to merge together to create something magical for self-sustaining community living. 'A tribe of women connected across the world that holds the space of conscious connection for the future of the new earth.'

This is the next story I am writing for myself ...

The next stage in my life is about how I can continue to support others in their own individual spiritual awakening journey. I feel that there is a gap in the client therapeutic process where there isn't the support for people experiencing a spiritual crisis and this is often labelled as a mental health issue. The world has consciously shifted and there has been a mass conscious awakening for humanity as a collective.

There are many people who need support on this journey. I feel that someone like myself, who has been on this path for fifteen years, has a lot of wisdom to share with others as a spiritual teacher and leader. I am a lightworker and this is my purpose and mission in this lifetime. I will continue to hold the light of conscious connection for planet earth and also support others experiencing a similar life journey.

Mea Allman

57 | From: Jamaica | Lives: Orlando, Florida

My culture is a big part of my life, from hearing stories from my mother of the past, present, and how it will transform and intertwine my future, from overcoming life challenges, joyful moments, to my survivorship journey.

This is who I am in the world ...

I'm a Caribbean woman who comes from a diverse mixed culture of Indo-Aryan (Bangladesh), Arawak Indian, Chinese, Costa Rican, Jamaican and Scotts. It's truly an honour to be born on 8 March, which is International Women's Day, that allows me to experience a part of a community that's my own.

In May 2000, I was faced with the biggest challenge, and that was being diagnosed with breast cancer. My joyful world became a nightmare and forced me to put on my big-girl panties and fight this fight. Although, during this fight I endured emotional challenges that led me to have thoughts of suicide. My mental illness journey towards the edge persisted until I realised that I wasn't crazy, I needed to get to the root of the problem by seeking help – which wasn't easy, opening up and letting all your demons out of the bag. This made me very vulnerable. I lost confidence, self-worth, I had weight management difficulties, depression and didn't want to live anymore.

I looked back to times of being bullied or shunned by people who did not understand my mixed cultural heritage and my difficulties in making friends. How in the world was I going to stop sitting and suffering in silence and get back my voice? What worked for me was realising that my strength came from within by taking back my power, something I call GLOW – my greater level of wellness within the mind, body and soul. I realised that those three entities had to be balanced and synchronised in harmony in order to exist daily. But to do this I had to dare myself by looking in the mirror and face the image I feared the most (self) – the demons inside of me were the root of the problems. Otherwise, I was in danger of diving off the edge into the abyss. I learned that instead of sitting in silence, I had to talk to someone, like a mental health professional, a life coach or other resources available. Today, I still battle with mental illness due to ongoing health issues after cancer, but I am at a place of mental wellness and love this beautiful woman I see in the mirror every day. I'm also a twenty-two-year cancer survivor … a warrior of hope and courage.

Having a second chance in life, I wanted to find purpose in my survivorship by making a difference. It was after attending the Orlando Carnival in May 2007 that I realised we dress in our island colours, but don't know our cultural history, national symbols or the meaning of the colours in the flag. Right there, a light bulb went off in my head that I needed to educate my Caribbean people. That led to the birth of *Karibbean Under One Magazine* in April 2008 to celebrate multiculturalism, feature interviews, how to live a healthier lifestyle, but most of all become acquainted with the richness of our cultural heritage.

But something in my life was still missing and not just my cultural passion. I wanted to raise awareness about breast cancer. In 2014, I created 'Ribbons of Survivors 365', to celebrate those who are survivors or still battling illnesses/conditions.

I not only wanted to raise awareness, but create a community for those to network, share testimonies and self-care tips and be a support system to help the next person. Today, Ribbons of Survivors 365 raises awareness beyond cancer.

This is the next story I want written for women …

Looking back to age seventeen – being bullied and culturally discriminated against for being mixed race, a Caribbean girl who spoke with a Jamaican/Canadian accent – my next mission was to create 'Women of Kulture 365', to help women navigate a world where they could feel open speaking with their cultural accent and use this to educate and share the richness of our culture. Each year in March I celebrate Women's History Month and International Women's Day, with an event entitled 'Women Rising & Reaching Back', a luncheon to honour women from diverse cultures. We celebrate, share our achievements, how we've overcome challenges and self-care tips, to support each other by building a community of sisterhood as our sisters' keepers locally and worldwide.

I remember my mom saying that you just can't see the world from a child's point of view, but imagine a world where you can achieve anything your mind can conceive. So, during COVID-19 in 2020, I wanted to put my knowledge to use and became a certified life, health and nutrition coach, to encourage others to make, meet and exceed goals in both their personal and professional lives and live a healthier lifestyle. In February 2021, I launched *GLOW 365* – a greater level of wellness TV show, with three other women. Our guests are top experts in their field who share a new approach in how to find balance within the mind, body and soul.

This is the next story I am writing for myself ...

I want to continue striving, thriving and surviving as a God-fearing woman who's passionate about her accomplishments, help others to be on their journey of mental wellness, be grateful for your blessings, never stop mastering self-love and especially stop sitting in silence and being voiceless. I was honoured to receive the 2021 Congressional Award from Congressman Darren Soto in lieu of Caribbean Heritage Month (June), which is documented and recorded in the Library of Congress for my accomplishments as community leader within Central Florida. I'm also an executive producer, broadcast journalist, cultural/health advocate and self-empowerment educator who's been reborn with a renewed life. My culture is a big part of my life, from hearing stories from my mother of the past and present, and how it will transform and intertwine my future, from overcoming life challenges, joyful moments to my survivorship journey as a Women of Kulture 365. Second chances don't come often, so cherish this life to the fullest.

Karli Bree

40 | From: Bacchus Marsh, Victoria, Australia | Lives: Bacchus Marsh, Victoria, Australia

You were never meant to hide, change or numb the person you were born as. You were meant to embrace yourself wholeheartedly and everything that makes you, YOU.

'But not anymore, not anymore now,
I'm not going to buy in, not going to buy in,
I'm kickin' you out and kicked you to the curb now,
I've found a better way, it won't go, it's here to stay.'
– An excerpt from Kaleidoscope by Karli Bree, 2012

This is who I am in the world ...

I am Karli Bree. I am a singer/songwriter, and this is a verse from one of my songs that I wrote at the height of my depression, as I let go of my addictions and embarked on a quest to find long-lasting happiness.

Over my life, I have felt that I never fitted in. I feel things more deeply than others; I can feel the pain of the world and a happiness that I sometimes cannot contain. I had anxiety from a young age and used food to numb these uncomfortable feelings and mask the pain of just being me. As I grew older, I included alcohol, drugs, sex, people-pleasing, perfectionism, abusive relationships and anger. In my thirties, after having a breakdown, I sadly thought suicide would end my pain.

I am now a music and yoga teacher, music therapist, musician, singer/songwriter, sound healer, breathwork practitioner, animal and nature communicator and a never-ending truth seeker.

Here is a little about my journey from darkness into the light ...

My healing journey began when I travelled to the island of Mentawai, Indonesia, venturing eight hours down a river in a canoe to live with an Indigenous tribe, embracing their simple lifestyle and zest for life. I lived the way they did and even got the traditional Mentawai tattoos, which remind me daily of this incredible experience and the time I spent with this beautiful tribe. I re-found my voice here, as the tribe's people revelled in my singing and playing guitar, I had a profound connection with the mumma of the tribe who helped me remember the amazing person I was.

I then travelled to India on my own for a vipassana retreat, where I sat with the voices in my head and uncomfortable bodily sensations. Through this, I found that, with patience, they disappear on their own, learning not to try to cover them up or shut them out as I had done with my addictions.

In Thailand in 2018, I undertook my yoga teacher training two-hundred-hour certification. Here I experienced new things that forever changed me for the better like ecstatic dance, kirtans, breathwork, kambo and ayahuasca ceremonies. These helped me to release trauma in my body.

Once home I knew there was a 'missing piece' in my healing puzzle which was hidden in my childhood where trauma lied. A therapist friend spoke to me about a trial called 'psilocybin therapy' involving the ingestion of mushrooms to help you journey back to a traumatic event. I journeyed to a time where I was eight years old and got bitten by a dog. I saw the incident from a different perspective and got the answers I needed to move on, to love the facial scars that this incident caused and see the gift in gaining tools around dealing with trauma and being okay with imperfections.

In 2020 I experienced a spontaneous Kundalini awakening, which was the final turning point as it broke down the barriers standing in my way for ultimate healing. This was the hardest thing that I have been through as it brought up a deep, constant fear of death. Through this awakening, I had the realisation of who I am and it allowed me to get rid of the self-confined patterns that no longer served me.

My Kundalini awakening continued for a year, and through a lot of patience, meditation, crystal work, energy healing, yoga, breathwork and other spiritual modalities, I have now come out the other side stronger than ever. I now feel as though I have found my soul's purpose, which is sharing ALL the things I have learnt in my healing journey so I can help others on their paths as well.

Vipassana cleared my mind, Thailand cleansed my body and the Kundalini awakening healed my heart.

This is the next story I want written for women ...

I want women to know that you were never meant to hide, change or numb the person you were born as. You were meant to embrace yourself wholeheartedly and everything that makes you, YOU, and it's never too late to start.

Stop trying to change all the wonderful things that make you, you. God made you EXACTLY how you are for a reason. There's not one, and never will be another, beautiful soul exactly like YOU.

The world needs you and what you have to offer. Own your story, as I have, and all the things that have led you up until this point as they could be the exact reason why you are here on your life's mission.

It's time now to let our light shine.

This is the next story I am writing for myself ...

As I am now able to share from the light, I celebrate all parts of me and all that I have found.

After many years of trying to change who I was, I now realise I am just a highly sensitive person and a full-blown empath, and that's okay … Just because you stop and talk to trees on your walks doesn't mean I have to stop! God made me this way for a reason, and I'm grateful.

I am now on a lifelong mission to help people find unshakable self-love and turn inwards to heal the parts of themselves that feel broken, so they don't need to cover them up with external things, to live a life of freedom and love from the inside out, instead of the outside in. To return home to themselves, remembering who they were before life and comparison got in the way.

Ten years ago I finished writing my song *Kaleidoscope*.
'A kaleidoscope is a constantly changing pattern or sequence of objects.'
My life journey, like a kaleidoscope, is just about to turn and begin again.
And I can't wait.

Megan Rose

33 | From: Jacksonville, Florida | Lives: Sugar Grove, North Carolina

I came into this world full of the sins of my ancestors but I will leave this world full of hope in our shared humanity, the arch of justice, and prayers of children when they're hunting for change to buy treats from the ice cream truck.

As an occupational therapist, I help people use their bodies as tools for regulation and their daily routines as rituals to create connection and meaning, giving me great joy to help someone live a full and peaceful life. I spend my days assessing children's experiences within their family, society and culture and then write long boring medical documents to beg insurance to pay me to help these families find peace. I wrote my stories below as a direct contrast to my daily monotony. With an overpriced degree and too much confidence for an unladylike southern American woman, I have only endless questions. I learn more from failure, antagonists and broken promises than anything else.

It has taken me thirty-three years to learn how to surround myself with people that fill me up instead of drain me dry, thirty years to be honest about who I am as a queer woman to my family and twenty-seven years to be honest with myself about what love means. It took escaping an abusive marriage, many friendship break-ups, the loss of a religious community and possibly the loss of my sanity to find myself. Ever since I started blindly feeling through the messy world around me, trusting the gut I was told not to follow, things have started turning out pretty good. I'll keep writing cheeky prose from my happy little holler in the Appalachian Mountains with my stinky bulldog at my feet and tender-hearted bear of a human at my side.

This is who I am in the world ...
Self-Prose

I am an asshole.

Born an animal, full of minerals.

I have pivoted between predator and prey.

Often mistaken.

While hoping for the best in people, I often fall for their worst.

Overly sensitive, opinionated and visceral.

Deeply empathetic but bursting at the seams with my own personal shit. I am full of rotten eggs, change of plans and empty promises.

Privileged and often out of sync.

I lost the directions and am going nowhere important.

I have been boundary-less and lost at sea.

I've been without a tool in a carpenter's workshop.

Up shit creek with only my hand for a paddle.

I've been everywhere and nowhere all at once – disassociated.

A mother's helper and a family's friend.

I am steel and stardust, love and light.

This brain swirls with an aurora borealis of colour and the rhythm of an old broken-down jukebox.

It is hard for me to focus on the words pouring from your mouth while I am distracted by the longing in your heart.

This body holds a scorecard for a game I've never asked to play.

This heart contains the emotional depth of all the ancestors that came before me.

I am a messy soul, a deep feeler, a queer woman and hopeful wreck trying to survive in a world that wasn't made for someone like me.

This is the next story I want written for women ...
The May Someday Prayer

Someday people will learn to use their bodies as tools for regulating their nerves, settling their minds and soothing their souls.

May their daily routines become rituals to create connection and meaning in their everyday lives.

Someday all humans will remake their worlds and we will not have to worry about the safety of a body based on their gender or non-gender expression.

May everyone's lived experience exist on a spectrum as wide and as varied as all other living species on this gorgeous planet.

Someday may our planet be covered in diverse forests in all their happy, healthy glory. May we always aim to exist on tree time.

Someday we will rewrite the stories that have been scribbled on our consciousness, our bodies, our very genomes.

May we learn that systems are made to support and connect us, not compare and compress us.

Someday the variety of our genetic expression, the shape of our bodies and the ebb and flow of a human life will be celebrated instead of scrutinised.

May all those suffering from disconnection of body, mind and spirit put down the measuring stick society shoved up their asses at birth.

Someday the principle of scarcity will die so that people can open their eyes to the abundance all around them.

May we release our fears and follow our curiosities into a more just and balanced world. May 'someday' come in our lifetimes.

This is the next story I am writing for myself ...

My Plan

To continue to get lost in the small, delightful moments of everyday life like: washing dishes in warm soapy water after preparing a delicious meal for the people I love; wandering in the woods with my dog searching for flora, fauna and healing; soul-searching conversations with good friends late into the night around a backyard fire; the sensation of bare feet clinging to mossy rocks while standing in the middle of a flowing river; scraping out the dirt from under my fingernails as I wash my hands after an afternoon of putting down roots; responding in balance to the flow of life around me instead of reacting from a place of hurt; nourishing and growing my taproot that grounds me to this mountain community; finding community in places far and wide from our place of origin; and *slowing the fuck down* and living on tree time.

Daily reminders that I am bad-ass at life pivots and every choice I have had the privilege to make has brought me to this lovely moment. Learning that the only things that have any real value in life come slowly, deliberately and require all your power.

Breathing deeply the smell of pine trees, morning mountain fog, creeks after a hard rain, a fresh cup of loose-leaf tea, wet paint on white canvas, the back of my partner's neck first thing in the morning, the furry wrinkles on my dog's thick neck and a spring forest on a lazy sunny afternoon.

I came into this world full of the sins of my ancestors, but I will leave this world full of hope in our shared humanity, the arch of justice and prayers of children when they're hunting for change to buy treats from the ice cream truck.

Michelle Berger

46 | From: Campbelltown, New South Wales, Australia | Lives: Huskisson, New South Wales, Australia

As I step into my power, I heal the generations that come before and after. I go first and bring other women along with me.

This is who I am in the world ...

Titles: daughter, loving partner, sister, aunt, teacher.

Trade: Bachelor (early childhood) working with children zero to five and their families for over twenty years.

Soul work: mediation facilitator working with chakras, sound, aroma and movement. Women's empowerment through our cycles and seasons.

I am an eternal student and love learning. Outdoor environments are medicine, where I feel the most nourished. I love music and dancing. I am super introverted and highly sensitive. I love ritual and ceremony, creating presence and meaning in the everyday. I am a great listener and will lend an ear and a shoulder to cry on anytime.

I grew up fully embodying the 'good girl' persona. Growing up, I unconsciously learnt to dull my light and be a dutiful daughter as my parents' energy was often focused on my rebellious younger sister. I was more concerned with being the 'good one'. I have always followed the rules, done the 'right thing' and been silent for most of my life in order to keep the peace and make others happy.

Now in my mid-forties, I am DEEP in transition, shedding the layers of conditioning that our patriarchal society dumps on girls and women. I question everything. I'm learning to use my voice. Speak my truth. Be unapologetically me. Even when I wobble. *Especially* when I wobble.

It's freaking hard and so empowering. Remembering my magic, rewilding the woman that has been pushed to conform in a system that does not understand the creatrix that is WOMAN.

My rewilding began about six years ago when I attended my first women's circle. I had been yearning to connect with other women, and when I saw a notice for a local circle, I instantly felt called to attend.

I didn't say a word that night other than my name during introductions, but I sat in utter awe of the courage and vulnerability of the other women as they shared their personal stories, struggles, triumphs and deep, deep traumas. I remember thinking at the time that I didn't deserve to sit alongside these incredible women because I didn't have a story to tell. Still, I left that night transformed, feeling like I had come home. I felt like I had been sitting with them my whole life, and I returned to that circle and those women each month and my journey of remembering and rewilding began.

Believing in myself and my worth has been a recurring theme throughout my life. Not believing I belong, always dimming my light to try and fit in, withdrawing from situations and relationships to avoid hurt and challenge and not trusting myself or the world to support and protect me.

As I continue my own rewilding, I have come to realise that I, too, have a story to share. I have gifts and a voice, and owning my story allows other women to do the same. As I step into my power, I heal the generations that come before and after. I go first and bring other women along with me, so we remember and rewild together. Our stories connect us in profound ways. That is where our magic lies – in sharing story, in connection and collaboration.

Another significant piece of my rewilding has been reconnecting to my monthly cycle. My monthly bleed has always brought debilitating pain, discomfort, embarrassment and dread. It has been fascinating to learn that our monthly cycle is representative of the four seasons and that we cycle through these each and every month. I am learning to support myself and my body by honouring each season in my cycle each month. The misinformation and lack of education about our monthly cycles is heartbreaking, but I am hopeful that women are being reintroduced to this wisdom and that I may be part of this rewilding for women.

This is the next story I want written for women ...
Right now, I am passionate about the rewilding of all women from the time they are young girls, who are taught that our value comes from within and we do not need to seek it outside ourselves. That we are powerful, resilient, magical and thrive in an environment of support and community, not competition, isolation and disconnection. That we are given space, support and encouragement to be all that we can be, to follow our dreams and our passions, instead of conforming to an ideal of what others think we should be.

That we are taught to love our bodies and honour our monthly cycles and seasons. That we are given the space to live by our seasons and energy and not see our cycle as a liability or something to be ashamed of or ignored, instead honouring the incredible vessel that gives life, nourishment and love to all. That we are taught to remember the wisdom of nature and reconnect to the land, plants and animals for nourishment and medicine.

That we reconnect to the sacred feminine and we sit in circle. That we reconnect to the sustenance and nourishment of the feminine collective, so we remember we are not alone, that we all have similar struggles and fears and that we work better in connection and community.

This is the next story I am writing for myself ...
I live lightly and love fiercely, continuing my rewilding. I yearn for more simplicity and a return to nature, living off the land by her seasons and cycles. I want to connect with the land I was born on and was never really taught about.

I want to re-engage with the cycles and seasons of my own body and Mama Nature as we sync together and support each other in each stage of our shared life cycle. Honouring the magic that is my body and my innate natural state of being, loving all parts of me and to live more consciously.

I now envision leading women in circle myself, developing deep soul connections with my fellow sisters. Supporting them to reconnect to themselves, their bodies and each other using ritual, ceremony, connection and celebration via heart-centred education programs and interactions with the natural world.

Dear sisters, let's remember and rewild together OX

Nathalie Banaszak

37 | From: Sweden | Lives: Bali, Indonesia

Your dreams wouldn't live within your heart if you didn't have the capacity and audacity to fulfill them.

'I have never tried that before, so I think I should definitely be able to do that.' – Pippi Longstocking

This is who I am in the world ...

Have you ever heard about Pippi Longstocking? She is a brilliant and original icon of girl power in a children's adventure series written by a Swedish author, showing us how to be unapologetically ourselves while courageously carving our own paths.

As a little girl, I LOVED Pippi, she was my hero to the point where I even told people that my name was Pippi. I clearly lived myself into her character vividly – she definitely didn't 'fit into a box', she owned her uniqueness and was clearly having much FUN.

Growing up, somewhere along the way, I lost the connection to that fierce Pippi power and my heart's voice. That's when I began to pay a lot of attention to what others were doing, what I felt I *should* do, how I *should* look and how I *should* be.

After almost reaching burnout while climbing the career ladder doing all the things that I was 'supposed' to do, I reached a point where I felt as if I had lost my inner spark and zest for life. Things had to dramatically change, and I knew that deep within.

I decided to take a huge leap of faith and quit my promising job to do the one thing my heart kept telling me to do – *I just want to travel the world and feel ALIVE again.*

I believe it was an inner yearning to go on a quest to find my own truth and be free.

Leaving the safe and familiar is never easy; it takes something and requires us to be brave and 'different'. Quitting my corporate job was a defining moment for me and the beginning of something else. A new life built from a place of love, joy and freedom – instead of fear.

My biggest learnings have come through a lot of failing forward and an ultimate LETTING GO of others' opinions and approval. And through giving my whole self space to take an honest look at the limiting beliefs I had living inside me that was dictating my life.

Looking back, I thought I was free when I was travelling the world. Today, freedom has a much deeper meaning to me – it means freedom of self. To be free to LIVE my life in colour every day as I want, expressing my whole and authentic self in heart alignment.

This is the next story I want written for women ...

Dear, brilliant woman! I want you to know this:

You have *unique* gifts, skills, talents and heart desires that are just waiting to be expressed and come alive. Your big dreams were planted in you for a reason; when you choose to tap into them and your authentic power, you will realise that you are *limitless.*

Your dreams wouldn't live within your heart if you didn't have the capacity and audacity to fulfil them. When YOU give yourself permission to live your full potential and shine your light unapologetically, you will inspire others to do the same.

Because …

Who are you NOT to shine bright?

When you take a bold stand for who you truly are and who you are here to become and LIVE your truth, you will become a force of light. The magic is to be found in your unique story, your mess and whatever challenges you've experienced.

All obstacles are assignments for you to rise above. That's how you develop resilience, gain wisdom and step into heart-aligned living. When you move beyond everything that's holding you back and keeping you small, it will set you free so you can soar.

I've been on a long journey to break free from who I thought I needed to be so that I could do the one most important thing I believe we all need to do. I gave myself PERMISSION to be who I truly am, show what I stand for and express myself freely.

My own mess and the fact that I decided to not only embrace all the old limiting stories I had living inside me, but to wholeheartedly deal with them, is the reason that I am who I am today. I'm passionate about helping other women transform and do the same.

This is the next story I am writing for myself ...

As a success coach and mentor, I help women to expand and become who they most want to be through personal transformation. I am massively passionate about seeing other women grow and unleash their uniqueness and full potential.

I deeply believe that when you invest in the brand called YOU through dedication, inner work and a commitment to change, you're also creating a meaningful and positive impact collectively. Because as you awake, rise and expand, so will the world.

The older I get and the more I learn, the more I realise there is to learn. I see myself as a humble student of life, committed to my own growth and healing. My intention is to be bolder, freer and to BE more ME every day than I was even yesterday.

While empowering heart-driven women to rise and step into their authentic power as we together rewrite the rules and create a new narrative of what success looks like. *Showing what fierce women as a leading force look like to create a global impact.*

On a philanthropic level, I aspire to educate and empower young girls with big dreams to embrace their authentic selves while expanding their thinking and mindset so that they fully can understand, embody and own the fact that *girls can BE and DO anything.*

I keep embodying aspects of Pippi Longstocking into the woman I choose to be in the world today. This joyous, loving, courageous and bold little girl keeps inspiring me into the next evolution of me while I continue to grow and carve my own unique path to living my purpose.

This I know for sure: When you lean back toward what lights you up and let JOY be the ultimate creator, you don't need to know all the how's on the journey toward your vision. Believe in yourself and your big dreams wholeheartedly – and trust the process.

Give yourself permission to shine.

Lisa Cybaniak Gustafsson

47 | From: Canada | Lives: England

Know when to lay down your sword or use it to cut ties. It is time to step into your power.

This is who I am in the world ...

After surviving a decade of child abuse, from psychological and physical to sexual, my teen years found me safe from my abuser but in danger from myself. Because of the words and actions of another person, I truly believed I was stupid, ugly, worthless and useless, nobody would ever love me and I would never be anything to this world.

I honestly believed that someone else needed to come along and show me my value. Of course, that was never going to happen – not because I was not valuable, but because I did not believe I had any. Therefore, anytime someone was kind to me, I assumed it must be because they wanted something from me or were laughing at me behind my back. I simply could not accept love or kindness from another person. In fact, most times I could not even see that it was there.

I spent a long time looking for someone else to save me from my torture, and since I always came up short, I was in constant pain. I wanted the pain to end so badly that for a few years I thought the only way to make that happen was to end my life. Luckily, somewhere deep in the back of my being, I knew that was not the answer – I needed to transcend this. I just did not know how.

Once I realised that this was what I would experience for the rest of my life if I did not do something about it, I went on a healing mission. I was not trying to heal from my child abuse – I was still in denial that that was even impacting my life. I was trying to find the meaning of it all. Why would I be made to suffer in such a way? What was so wrong with me that this is what I deserved?

What I learned was more than I could ever imagine back then. I began to explore the concept of spirituality – life after death, reincarnation, the purpose we set for ourselves in each life. And that changed everything! The idea that I was in control of choosing when and where I reincarnated and who would be my parents really began to replace that sense of disempowerment over my life with control – something I felt I never had.

But when I realised that I chose all the major players in my life to help me learn my lessons, that is when true empowerment set in. It is also when my entire perspective on my life shifted. Up until this point, I had lived my whole life believing my lesson was that I was worthless. Now, I understood that I would never incarnate into a life to learn a lesson like that – nobody would! So, if that was not my lesson, what was?

This is the moment that changed everything because this is when I realised my lesson was to find my worth; to love and accept myself. And because I found my way to this understanding through the concept of reincarnation and soul purpose, I already was shifting into a deep respect for myself. Instead of feeling like a helpless victim to my abuser and my life, I now had clarity and power. And with me back in the driver's seat of my own life, I was in control. I could choose anything I wanted – and I wanted to love and accept myself.

I know now I am the goddess of ancestral wisdom and universal connection. I am the divine feminine balanced with the divine masculine, here to experience life in human form so I can understand myself more fully. My purpose is to help others use their experiences as catalysts in their evolution, while doing the same to allow for my ascension. I am a catalyst for change, growth and acceptance of oneself, just as you are in this moment. And I am dedicated to helping others find their own way through bespoke programs and courses using belief clearing, reiki and neurolinguistic programming (NLP).

As a priestess of the goddess in all her forms and descendant of Odin, god of healing and of war, I understand the battle we face is within. It is equally important to know when to lay down our sword or use it to cut ties. It is time to step into your power.

This is the next story I want written for women ...

The divine feminine lives in you. You ARE divine. We are one. Anything and everything you could ever want, you already have. In fact, it IS YOU. It is time to connect with your true self – your higher self – once more and do what you have come here to do. For too long you have walked in the shadows; you have thought and planned too small as you had forgotten who you are. You, sister, were meant for greatness. You, sister, ARE greatness.

This is the next story I am writing for myself ...

As I continue to evolve, I help millions of other women do the same. I follow my path, surrendering to the flow of life – to the very universe that we all are. I listen to my intuition and the signs that are all around me, guiding me. I am clearing my karmic debt from this life and others and releasing myself from vows and oaths that no longer serve me. I understand that I do not have to destroy my ego to grow. Rather, the ego society tells me to reject is just my *unhealed* ego. Just as her name suggests, she can be healed, and I celebrate the steps I take in that endeavour. And all along this path I take, I help others in finding and creating theirs by raising the vibrational energy of the planet and women across the globe.

Gail Carmody

From: Australia | Lives: Sydney, Australia

It is paramount that women be encouraged and taught how to develop and express confidence in their gender, sexuality, varying roles and positions they choose to have during their lifetime. To have the freedom of love, experience joy, fulfilment, meaning and to enjoy an uncompromised full human expression of self.

This is who I am in this world ...

I play many roles in this world which require me to adapt, pivot and learn constantly each day.

The most important role I play is a mother and grandmother to my daughter Laura and my two grandchildren Isabel and Henry.

I focus on ensuring that I am present and give my two most precious assets, time and love, to my grandchildren and daughter. Unfortunately, I did not understand the value of these assets when my daughter was younger.

I thought time was an endless resource, and I thought one day I would reduce my work hours, along with energy spent in the workplace and spend more time with her. Little did I realise how quickly those valuable years and time would go and that I would not be able to retrieve or regain any of this time.

I placed great value on developing a professional career, making a difference to the businesses I worked in. This was through abundantly giving unlimited time, energy, contributing unlimited skills and knowledge in my varying roles.

Unfortunately, I did not appreciate my true value of being me, and what I could contribute through being present and spending quality time with my immediate family, my daughter and husband.

This also included me not being present and having time for my parents in my role as a daughter and my siblings in my role as a sister. This also applied as an aunty, nurse and often as a friend. I have always been resilient and tenacious and focused on reaching my goals, rather than being present with others.

In the later years, through my continued learning and personal development and as a coach, I have now realised that my greatest role is being an example to all humans through using compassion, giving to others of my time, knowledge and love.

These learnings have taught me to slow down, share, enjoy, give to and love those I come across in all my roles in the world as I am today.

This is the next story I want written for women ...

The story I want written for women is for them to have a strong global presence with equality in all aspects of life. Experiencing life to the fullest whatever this may mean for each woman.

Equality encompasses many aspects of life and can mean different things in different cultures and societies. In general, this is equality in decision-making, speech, politics, education, access to food, clean water, health care. Including equality with human rights, freedom of speech and freedom of choice. Equality in the contribution and respect of the opinion of world affairs and major world decisions/events.

It is paramount that women be encouraged and taught how to develop and express confidence in their gender, sexuality and varying roles and positions they choose to have during their lifetime. To have the freedom of love, joy, fulfilment, meaning and to enjoy an uncompromised full human expression of self.

Most importantly, be free to make their own choices without prejudice, ridicule, religious, environmental or societal burden.

I would like the next story to read that all women have equality, self-confidence, self-respect and self-love, built on their individual financial security, financial acumen and freedom. This would be underpinned with self-acknowledgement of their individual and collective worth in their lives, roles, work, society, country and world.

How this is possible is through our children who are our future. They are our conduit and platform to create confidence, equality, respect, compassion, empathy, joy and peace in the world of tomorrow.

When I speak about equality it encompasses not only women, but all humankind, in all areas of life – physical, emotional, spiritual, cultural and environmental.

The responsibility for such change by our future generations starts with not only women today but by all who are instrumental in the early years of children's lives.

This includes multiple people such as parents, carers, teachers, relatives, religious and social influencers – anyone that has been given the privilege of being involved in raising children.

These people need to teach children through being present, listening, directing, demonstrating and facilitating life learning and questioning minds.

It is our responsibility to help make the difference through being the example to make the next story for women a generational continuum of human equality.

This is the next story I am writing for myself ...

The story I want to write for myself is to learn about myself, life and the importance of love, joy and human connection from an early childhood.

Including how to understand, learn and maintain self-confidence, respect and love and the importance of sharing this knowledge with others.

Particularly, my daughter, grandchildren, nieces and nephews, then to the wider community.

My future self will understand the true value of time as a resource and the importance of maximising and utilising it for the good of myself and others.

I have only gained an appreciation of the value of time as a resource in my later years. It is only now that I understand that I am unable to retrieve, retrace or reuse time. This is particularly so regarding my parents.

I thought time was an unlimited resource – never-ending – and I would spend time with them later.

As I reflect on this, I realise that later never came.

I will ensure that I am a beacon and shining example to humankind in demonstrating how important personal growth and continuous learning is to enable one to be fulfilled and lead to a meaningful life, as well as being present in all human connections.

Through a full knowledge and the correct skill set, I will experience financial and business success. I will continue as a role model for my grandchildren, through being present, continuing to give to others and teaching them the importance of truly embodying joy and peace in their lives. This, coupled with always giving self-acknowledgement and being responsible for all my choices.

My story will tell tales of extensive travel, experiencing new foods, people, languages, cultures and natural beauty.

Completed with a large, welcoming home to return to which will welcome limitless family and friends, full of laughter, joy, peace, giving and happiness.

Maybe completed with a loving partner!

Jasmine Gatt

30 | From: Sydney, Australia | Lives: Perth, Western Australia

My wish is that, just by taking a look at the artwork unfolding of who I am, that joy will flicker and grow within you. As by looking at me, you are looking at you, too.

This is who I am in the world ...

I am a constant evolution of self, continually learning, growing and expanding. Deepening my awareness and connection with self. Curious and hungry for more. I am a mother, a partner, a daughter. I am passionate, and I lead with my heart. I am intuitive, I am connected to my deep inner knowing. I am a guide for those seeking inner healing, enabling them to unlock the tools they've always had, yet sought permission to use. I am continuing to walk that very same path myself.

In the past I have based my value on labels and job descriptions. I learn best through experience. Practical, hands-on, sometimes 'the hard way', experience. I feel my way through things. I think and I dream, I create and I explore. I have been guilty of living in a dream state and not being present where I am at the time. Living a dream life, yet fantasising of what is next. *I will be happy when ...* Is the statement that I am learning to release, as what serves me best now is presence and experiencing life, in real time, as it is.

There have been two times in my life when I have stood back and thought, *How could I have possibly gotten myself into this situation?* Stuck and in despair.

At the time, I had only managed to recognise that health and happiness were my non-negotiables and priorities moving forward. It wasn't until over six years later, when I began my training as a self-love coach, that the exercise of self-forgiveness unveiled my true diagnosis. A deep-rooted desperation to be loved, so prominent, that I had turned a blind eye to pain.

When entering that new chapter of becoming a coach, my intention was to continue guiding and helping others. However, it was me who needed guidance. And so, the process of loving and accepting myself began.

The second experience for me that left me feeling stuck and in despair once again was the situation of COVID-19. I had lived a life of travel and excitement for over ten years prior. Again, building an identity of fun, success and adventure. Returning to Australia to be completely grounded, I realised that without my traveller identity, I didn't know who I was.

What has followed this chapter has been nothing short of divine. Some of the most magical pieces of my story have unfolded from this redirection. Collaboration, creation, love and gratitude.

My journey to self-love has been a journey home. Recognising that the permission and validation that I have previously sought is irrelevant. In fact, creating an identity to discover who I was, was all torn down to leave me with all that I had left – me. Relearning who I was without all of the noise, an experience that I continuously repeat, as I am always growing.

Learning to accept all parts of me, the ones I liked and the ones I hid. The experiences I remembered with pride and the ones that rattled me with fear. My journey to self-love evolved when I understood that the best path forward was the version of me that was integrated. That accepted all pieces and parts and embraced them as a whole.

I am an imperfect masterpiece that has only been partially painted. Some parts have been painted over, other parts have been left bare. Yet all in all, you can see the story as it unfolds on the canvas, and as complicated and open to interpretation as this piece is, it emanates joy. My wish is that, just by taking a look at the artwork unfolding of who I am, joy will flicker and grow within you. As by looking at me, you are looking at you, too.

This is the next story I want written for women ...

Confidence and curiosity, never fearing the unknown. For women to feel empowered to be bold and adventurous, and for their individual uniqueness to be encouraged. For the duality of femininity and masculinity to be embodied and integrated within us all. Allowing for periods of rest and nourishment, without the guilt and shame of enacting the feminine.

For the seasons when inspiration is plentiful and inspired action is present, to be accepted as the norm, to stand in our masculinity. To work with the seasons and chapters of life.

To joyfully collaborate and co-create our lives. Lives that we are proud of, where love is the primary currency and happiness is the predominant energy. Where flow is normal, and stagnation is released.

This is the next story I am writing for myself ...

To turn within when searching. Leading a life that requires external validation and answers that are beyond me is no longer of service. To enjoy the duality of speeding up and slowing down, to embrace that both have their place, and to enjoy this without guilt or judgement.

I am aware that as I write out what I dream my future to be, as it approaches it will all change, because so do I. Always gathering, evolving and experiencing – trusting that I no longer appreciate things as a destination. Instead, I relish the journey.

I live as a guide, helping people connect with who they are, and I am continually reminded to reconnect with myself too.

I appreciate that becoming the best version of me serves those around me. That living a life I love gives permission to the ones that I hold dear to do the same for themselves.

I endeavour to continue creating, to allow passion and love to lead the way forward. To grow into the mother that my children need, to the supportive and motivating being that my partner desires, to the comfort and support that my family and friends appreciate, and to the inspirational and impactful woman that the child within me always dreamt that I would become.

I am choreographing a beautiful dance with life in each moment. Combining all of my favourite people and things, and creating the most wonderful and satisfying balance. I live and I learn to love each and every day, fully and present.

Epilogue

I do hope that you have really enjoyed *55 FACES!*

55 FACES forms part of *The Aspire Series,* a global platform for women who are leading change and impact through the lens of connection, expression and leadership. We do this through exploring narrative – our life stories and wisdom, heart and soul connection to self, others and humanity through social change, impact and how we exist in the broader scheme of things.

It is my belief that there is a sweet spot between each of these parts where we as women can write, review and rewrite our stories and the more established narratives that influence us, guiding the way for our communities and beyond. With a gentle footprint, we can make a bold impact and leave this place better than we found it, because of who we are and how we are with one another.

The Aspire Series hosts a series of short and longer courses, programs, events and The Summit. Each is designed to support, encourage and grow women, offering them opportunities to expand their voice and step further into leadership.

You can learn more about *The Aspire Series* here:
theaspireseries.com
I am excited to chat with you,
Michelle x

www.ingramcontent.com/pod-product-compliance
Lightning Source LLC
Chambersburg PA
CBHW061131010526
44107CB00068B/2902